RUDE WIT

Published in 2012 by Prion
an imprint of the Carlton Publishing Group
20 Mortimer Street
London W1T 3JW

Text compilation copyright © 2012 Nick Holt
Design and layout © 2012 Carlton Books Ltd

ISBN: 978-1-85375-864-5
Printed in China

RUDE WIT

Over 800 of the cleverest and most
scathing putdowns ever uttered!

Nick Holt

PRION

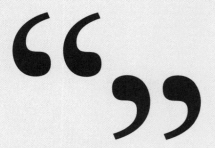

Haven't we all longed for that mot-juste when on the receiving end of an ear-bashing from a customer or client or colleague?

Haven't we all struggled for the right phrase when describing the inhuman inadequacy of our friends, our football team or the entire human race?

Haven't we all ached for the pithy one-liner to shrink the guy in the Porsche looking smug at the traffic lights?

Haven't we all dreamed of writing the ultimate scathing review of the piece of unspeakable garbage we were made to sit through at the cinema?

If this is you, then here is the answer to your prayers.

Contents

There are over 1,200 quotes in this collection. Each quote that appears is numbered (i.e. •123). These numbers run sequentially throughout the book. Use the index at the back to find great exponents of the put-down. The index is listed in alphabetical order by surname.

If you haven't got anything good to say about anyone come and sit by me.

*Alice Roosevelt Longworth had this maxim embroidered upon a cushion;
in Michael Teague,* Mrs L: Conversations with Alice Roosevelt Longworth *(1981)* •1

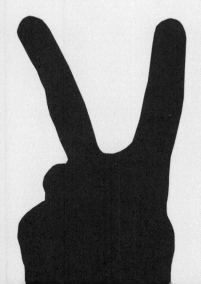

Judge: You are extremely offensive, young man.

Smith: As a matter of fact, we both are, and the only difference between us is that I am trying to be, and you can't help it.

Conservative politician and lawyer F.E. Smith, Lord Birkenhead; Earl of Birkenhead (1933) •2

I fart in your general direction! Your mother was a hamster and your father smells of elderberries.

Insulting French soldier in **Monty Python and The Holy Grail** *(1975)* •3

I hope all your children have very small dicks! And that includes the girls!

Jeff Goldblum as Dexter in **The Tall Guy** *(1989)* •4

She's as nervous as a very small nun on a penguin shoot.

Philip Glenister as Gene Hunt in **Life On Mars** •5

You are all camphire and frankincense, all chastity and odour.

William Congreve, **The Way of the World** *(1700)* •6

I regard you with an indifference closely bordering on aversion.

Robert Louis Stevenson, **New Arabian Nights** *(1882)* •7

Because thou art lukewarm and neither cold nor hot, I will spue thee out of my mouth.

Bible, Revelation 3.16 •8

Some men are born mediocre, some men achieve mediocrity, and some men have mediocrity thrust upon them, With Major Major it has been all three.

Joseph Heller, **Catch-22** *(1961)* •9

I am Holly, the ship's computer, with an I.Q. of 6000 — the same I.Q. as 6000 P.E. teachers.

Norman Lovett as Holly in **Red Dwarf,** 'Future Echoes' *1988* •10

The only gracious way to accept an insult is to ignore it; if you can't ignore it, top it; if you can't top it, laugh at it; if you can't laugh at it, it's probably deserved.

Russell Lynes, American writer and critic •11

If I throw a stick, will you leave?

Anon. •12

He waltzes like a Protestant curate.

Kate O'Brien, from **The Last of Summer** *(1943)* •13

One more push, I'm gonna to smack his face so hard he'll have to stick his toothbrush up his arse to clean his teeth!

Terence Stamp as Bernadette in **Adventures of Priscilla, Queen of the Desert** *(1994)* •14

No brilliance is needed in the law. Nothing but common sense, and relatively clean fingernails.

John Mortimer,
A Voyage Round My Father,
screenplay, *1972* •15

Let him be damned in his going and coming in. The Lord strike him with madness and blindness. May the heavens empty upon him thunderbolts and the wrath of the Omnipotent burn itself unto him in the present and future world. May the Universe light against him and the earth open to swallow him up.

Pope Clement VI (1478-1534)
invokes a happy prospect for
excommunicated sinners. •16

One should forgive one's enemies, but not before they are hanged.

Heinrich Heine •17

Hey, barkeep. Whose leg do you have to hump before you get a dry martini round here?

Brian, the dog from Family Guy •18

There is no sin except stupidity.

Oscar Wilde, 'The Critic as Artist' *(1891)* •19

'I am inclined to think — said I' [Dr Watson]. 'I should do so,' Sherlock Holmes remarked, impatiently.

Arthur Conan Doyle, **The Valley of Fear** *(1915)* •20

Clevinger was one of those people with lots of intelligence and no brains, and everyone knew it except those who soon found it out. In short, he was a dope.

Joseph Heller, Catch-22 *(1961)* •21

Mr Kremlin himself was distinguished for ignorance, for he had only one idea, — and that was wrong.

Benjamin Disraeli, Sybil *(1845)* •22

I don't think there's intelligent life on other planets. Why should other planets be any different from this one?

Bob Monkhouse, attrib., in BBC News December 2003 (online ed.) •23

The march of the human mind is slow.

Edmund Burke •24

We've all heard that a million monkeys banging on a million typewriters will eventually reproduce the entire works of Shakespeare. Now, thanks to the Internet, we know this is not true.

Robert Wilensky, in Mail on Sunday *February 1997* •25

You beat your pate,
  and fancy wit will come:
Knock as you please,
  there's nobody at home.

Alexander Pope, 'Epigram: You beat your pate' *(1732)* •26

He may look an idiot and talk like an idiot but don't let that fool you. He really is an idiot.

Groucho Marx •27

Oh dear, why does Lydia always come in — and why must she beg me to believe that she thinks seriously every day of her life, as she says? When her brain is a cage of canaries?

Virginia Woolf on the Russian ballerina Lydia Lopokova •28

It occurs to me that it takes a rather special sort of person to follow soaps. You have to be highly intelligent (to understand them) and as thick as a brick (to want to).

Alan Coren, **Mail On Sunday, 1986** •29

Squire: If I had a son who was an idiot, by Jove, I'd make him a parson!

Sydney Smith: Very probably, but I see that your father was of a different mind.

The Rev. Sydney Smith, wit, essayist and canon of St. Paul's Cathedral. •30

To call you stupid would be an insult
to stupid people.
I've known sheep
that could outwit
you; I've worn dresses
with higher IQs.
But you think you're
an intellectual,
don't you, ape?

Jamie Lee Curtis as Wanda in
A Fish Called Wanda *(1988)* •31

You couldn't pour piss out of a boot if the instructions were on the heel.

Lyndon Baines Johnson to a subordinate; in Robert Caro, The Years of Lyndon Johnson: Master of the Senate •32

I never forget a face, but in your case I'll be glad to make an exception.

Groucho Marx; in Leo Rosten, People I have Loved, Known or Admired *(1970),* 'Groucho' •33

19

Is that your face, or has your head just vomited?

Comedian Julian Clary deals with hecklers •34

He had the sort of face that makes you realise God does have a sense of humour.

Bill Bryson, Neither Here Nor There *(1991)* •35

My face looks like a wedding cake that has been left out in the rain.

W. H. Auden on himself •36

I kept thinking, if his face was that wrinkled, what did his balls look like?

David Hockney ponders the important questions after drawing W.H. Auden; attrib. •37

I've never seen anybody look so fucking ugly with just one head.
Peter Capaldi as Malcolm Tucker in **The Thick of It** •38

Twin miracles of mascara, her eyes looked like the corpses of two small crows that had crashed into a chalk cliff.
Clive James on a TV interview with Barbara Cartland, in the Observer, *August 1981* •40

We had the old Crow over at Hull recently, looking like a Christmas present from Easter Island.
Philip Larkin, of fellow poet Ted Hughes; letter, *1975* •39

It makes me look as if I were straining at a stool
Winston Churchill on his portrait by Graham Sutherland •41

Why did he [Onassis] marry that Jackie? She is ugly, with horrible legs, the skin of a hen, fat in the wrong places, and eyes too far apart from one another. She's a big nothing.
Aristotle Onassis finds a formidable opponent in Lisa Calogeropoulos, mother of his former mistress Maria Callas. •42

My face looks like a bouquet of elbows.

American comedian Phyllis Diller •43

Her manner has been described as that of a dominatrix, but with her practical cropped hair and glasses, she is more like a school librarian in a black leather coat. Her insults are innocuous.
The New York Times *on Anne Robinson's* **The Weakest Link** •44

About as cuddly as a cornered ferret.

Lynn Barber on Anne Robinson, in **The Times** *October 2001* •45

A cherub's face,
a reptile all the rest.

Alexander Pope, of Lord Hervey;
'An Epistle to Doctor Arbuthnot' *(1735)* •46

A red-haired, red-faced,
man of 65 seemingly in
transit between Dr Jekyll
and Mr Hyde.

Peter McKay on Paul Johnson,
in the Sunday Times,
November 1993 •48

He looked like
Rameses II with
his wrappings off.

Hugh Fullerton •47

He looked like an extra from
a crowd by Hieronymus Bosch.
Kenneth Tynan •49

He was there with two very worn and chipped looking ladies — the saddest looking remnants of ladies — in fact they reminded me of those cups without saucers that you sometimes see outside a china shop — all-on-this-tray-one-penny.

Katherine Mansfield •50

At least, she is not any worse-looking than she used to be in her youth; hers are features which never alter, unfortunately for her.

George Sand •51

Hunt: I think you've forgotten who you're talking to.

Tyler: An overweight, over-the-hill, nicotine-stained, borderline-alcoholic homophobe with a superiority complex and an unhealthy obsession with male bonding?

Hunt: You make that sound like a bad thing.

Philip Glenister and John Simm exchange banter as Gene Hunt and Sam Tyler in **Life On Mars** •52

Never trust a man who combs his hair straight from his left armpit.

Alice Roosevelt Longworth on 'the careful distribution of hair on General MacArthur's balding head'; *Michael Teague,* **Mrs L: Conversations with Alice Roosevelt Longworth** *(1981)* •53

Two bursts in a sofa.

Bobby Corbett describes the particularly hirsute armpits of a Wimbledon spectator; recalled in his obituary, **Daily Telegraph** *13 March 1999* •54

She looks like
she combs her hair
with an egg-beater.
Louella Parsons on Joan Collins •55

You can have affection for
a murderer or a sodomite, but
you cannot have affection for
a man whose breath stinks.
George Orwell •57

Why don't you
get a haircut?
You look like a
chrysanthemum.
P.G. Wodehouse •56

My Grandmother
took a bath every
year, whether she
needed it or not.
Brendan Behan •58

26

She looked like Lady Chatterley above the waist and the gamekeeper below.

Cyril Connolly, on Vita Sackville-West •59

You have sent me a Flanders mare.

Henry VIII when he saw Anne of Cleves, his fourth wife for the first time quoted by Tobias Smollett •61

This Englishwoman
is so refined
She has no bosom
and no behind.

**Stevie Smith,
'This Englishwoman'
(1937) •60**

One more facelift on this one and she'll have a beard.

Joanna Lumley as Patsy in Jennifer Saunders' Absolutely Fabulous •62

Her figure is corpulent, her complexion coarse, one eye gone, and her neck immense.

Lady Holland, on Lady Georgiana Spencer •63

She fitted into my biggest armchair as if it had been built around her by someone who knew they were wearing armchairs tight about the hips that season.

P.G. Wodehouse, My Man Jeeves (1919) •64

I'd kill myself if I was that fat.

Elizabeth Hurley ponders the charm of Marilyn Monroe. •65

I cannot believe the size of her butt. If she does appear in *Playboy*, it will have to be an extra big edition

Joan Collins on Monica Lewinsky. •66

[Alfred Hitchcock] thought of himself as looking like Cary Grant. That's tough, to think of yourself one way and look another.

Tippi Hedren, interview in California, 1982, in Boller and Davis, Hollywood Anecdotes *(1988)* •67

All these hands all over the place. You were like a sweaty octopus trying to unhook a bra.

Peter Capaldi as Malcolm Tucker in The Thick of It, *on a Minister's disastrous performance in a TV interview* •69

For God's sake, Walter, why don't you chop off her legs and read the rings?

Carol Matthau; in response to her husband's question regarding the age of a particularly thick-limbed starlet: in Truman Capote, Answered Prayers *(1986)* •68

He was so fat if he sat on a worm on a rock it would make a fossil in about five minutes. Then scientists wouldn't have to wait a million years.

Jane Hamilton •70

Lord Northcliffe: The trouble with you, Shaw, is that you look as if there were a famine in the land.
Shaw: The trouble with you, Northcliffe, is that you look as if you were the cause of it.

Playwright George Bernard Shaw, in an exchange with portly newspaper tycoon Lord Northcliffe (Alfred Charles William Harmsworth, 1865-1922) •71

In a New York bath house, where the practice for those wanting a partner was to leave the cubicle door open, a young man recoiled on seeing John Schlesinger's 'mound of flesh':

Anonymous: Oh, please. I couldn't. You've got to be kidding.
Schlesinger: A simple 'No' will suffice.

John Schlesinger, in Alan Bennett, diary 2003; in London Review of Books January 2004 •72

Naked, I had a body that invited burial.

Spike Milligan •73

My genitals are like a sort of travel version of Linford Christie's.

Frank Skinner •74

My best birth control now is to leave the lights on.

American comedienne Joan Rivers •75

Well, Nell, said she, presenting her cool peach cheek to me, how are you? Much the same as usual I see — hair arranged with a pitchfork and dress with a view to ventilation.

Rhoda Broughton •76

She wears her clothes
as if they were thrown
on her with a pitchfork.

Jonathan Swift,
Polite Conversation *(1738)* •77

Victoria Beckham gives
away all her old clothes to
starving children. Well who
else are they going to fit?

Pauline Calf •78

Cordelia: Willow! Hi. I like
   your outfit.
Willow: No, you don't.
Cordelia: No, I really don't.
   But I need a favour.
**Charisma Carpenter (Cordelia) and
Alyson Hannigan (Willow) in** Buffy the
Vampire Slayer, **'Prophecy Girl'** •79

Like a fist fight in a hydrangea bush.

*Craig Brown on buxom Dame Jill Knight
wearing a floral print* •80

Englishwomen's shoes look
as if they had been made
by someone who had often
heard shoes described,
but had never seen any.

Margaret Halsey, 1938 •81

Miss Strozzi… had the temerity to wear as truly horrible a gown as I have ever seen on the American stage. There was a flowing skirt of pale chiffon — you men don't have to listen — and a bodice of rose-coloured taffeta, the sleeves of which extended shortly below her shoulders. Then there was an expanse of naked arms, and then, around the wrists, taffeta frills such as are fastened about the unfortunate necks of pretend white poodle-dogs in animal acts. Had she not luckily been strangled by a member of the cast while disporting this garment, I should have fought my way to the stage and done her in myself.

Dorothy Parker reviews **Kay Strozzi** *in* **The Silent Witness,** *in* **The New Yorker,** *1931* •82

A brilliant blue garment that was an offence alike to her convictions and her complexion.

Edith Somerville and Martin Ross, **Further Experiences of an Irish R.M.** *(1908)* •83

Perhaps the Majors and the Blairs and all the power-dressers of Britain should take the advice of Wallis Simpson to the Queen Mother who, when asked how she could best promote British fashion abroad, replied crisply: Stay at home.

From **The Wit and Wisdom of the Royal Family** •84

> She made her look like a lampshade in a curry house.

Journalist Andrew Marr responds to reports that 'style guru' Carole Caplin was responsible for dressing President Putin's wife for the Russian state visit; in Daily Telegraph *July 2003* (online ed.) •85

> Now I know the meaning of the word 'grotesque'.

Sydney Smith, on seeing Mrs Grote in a huge rose-coloured turban; Peter Virgin, Sydney Smith *(1994)* •86

> The Pope. Great guy. But in a fashion sense, he's one hat away from being the Grand Wizard of the Ku Klux Klan.

Jon Stewart •87

Christian Dior's New Look consists of clothes by a man who doesn't know women, never had one, and dreams of being one.
Coco Chanel •88

In appearance Dior is like a bland country curate made out of pink marzipan.

Cecil Beaton describes legendary couturier Christian Dior; **The Glass of Fashion** *(1954)* •89

Noël Coward: You look almost like a man.
Edna Ferber: So do you.
Noël Coward, to Edna Ferber — who was wearing a tailored suit •90

When a woman looks at a man in evening dress, she sometimes can't help wondering why he wants to blazon his ancestry to the world by wearing a coat with a long tail to it.
Helen Rowland •91

One thing I've learned from both Star Trek and Moonbase is that men are going to be wearing simple pullovers for ever. I never did think that all that shoulder padding forecast by Hollywood in its science fiction would really catch on. I've also learned, not to my surprise, that women will continue to sport minis and plenty of décolletage whatever the stardate.

Bernard Hollowood in **Punch,** *September 1973* •92

Until Eve gave him the apple, [Adam] didn't even know he wasn't wearing underpants.

Paula Yates •93

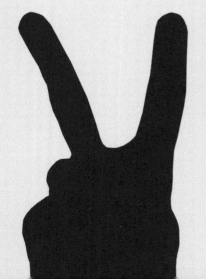

Nature intended women to be our slaves... they are our property; we are not theirs. They belong to us, just as a tree that bears fruit belongs to a gardener. What a mad idea to demand equality for women!... Women are nothing but machines for producing children.

Napoleon Bonaparte •94

Nature, I say, doth paynt them further to be weak, fraile, impacient, feble, and foolishe; and experience hath declared them to be unconstant, variable, cruell, and lacking in the spirit of counsel and regiment.

John Knox, **The First Blast of the Trumpet Against the Monstrous Regiment of Women** *(1558)* •95

A woman without a man is like a fish without a bicycle.

Gloria Steinem; attrib. •96

The 'g' is silent. The only thing about her that is.

Journalist Julie Burchill on self-styled feminist bisexual egomaniac Camille Paglia; in The Spectator, *1992* •97

All this Women's Liberation noise, I'm for it, of course — what I'm against is their idea that they invented it.

Katherine Hepburn •98

Whatever women do they must do twice as well as men to be thought half as good. Luckily, this is not difficult.

Charlotte Whitton (1896-1975), former mayor of Ottowa. •99

Well, I've finally figured out that being male is the same thing, more or less, as having a personality disorder.
Carol Shields •100

Maleness remains a recessive genetic trait like colour—blindness and haemophilia.
Elizabeth Gould Davies •101

Dullards, malingerers, gigolos, sycophants, boors — and that's the best of them… betrayers all. None of them worth the socks they stick their big feet into.
American novelist Lucy Ellmann •102

How often the Gods endow a man with a perfect profile and no brains to live up to it.
Katherine Mansfield •103

I think men are very funny.
If I had one of those dangly
things stuffed down the front
of my pants, I'd sit at home
all day laughing at myself.

Dawn French •104

Are you my alternative?

*Florynce R. Kennedy responds to a heckler
who asked if she was a lesbian.* •106

Men can read maps
better than women.
'Cos only the male
mind could conceive
of one inch equalling
a hundred miles.

Roseanne Barr •105

Sam: I've never met
an intelligent woman
I'd want to date.
Diane: On behalf of
all the intelligent women
in America, may I
just say… whew!

Ted Danson and Shelley Long in Cheers•107

> [Some guys] make love like they were the only ones in the room, which I think is a holdover from when they were.
>
> *Diane Nichols* •108

Henry: I'm trying to fill in one of these National Lottery tickets. I thought I'd put down the number of times I had sex last month, but they don't go higher than 49.
Joy: Try sticking to the number of times someone else was there.
David Swift and Susannah Doyle in Drop the Dead Donkey •109

Like having a large wardrobe fall on top of you with the key still in the lock.

A former girlfriend's description of being made love to by Nicholas Soames; in Gyles Brandreth, **Breaking the Code** *(1999)* •110

Roseanne went on
Saturday Night Live
and said I had a 3-inch
penis. Well, even a 747
looks small if it's landing
in the Grand Canyon.

Tom Arnold •111

Remember,
you're fighting
for this woman's
honour, which is
probably more
than she ever did.

*Groucho Marx as Firefly
in* **Duck Soup***(1933)* •113

You were born with your legs
apart. They'll send you to the
grave in a Y—shaped coffin.

Joe Orton, **What the Butler Saw** *(1969)* •112

She has been kissed as often as a police-court Bible, and by much the same class of people.
Robertson Davies •115

Here lies all that
   remains of Charlotte,
Born a virgin, died
   a harlot.
For sixteen years she
   kept her virginity,
A marvellous thing for
   this vicinity.
Anonymous epitaph
found in Welland,
Ont. •114

She's had more hands up her dress than the Muppets.

Joan Rivers on her fictional character, Heidi Abromowitz •117

Frasier: Oh, dad, she's not a weirdo. She's just a woman who finds me utterly fascinating.

Niles: And the distinction would be?

Kelsey Grammer and David Hyde Pierce in Frasier *•116*

Her legs were apart so often they were pen pals.

Joan Rivers embellishes the reputation of her fictional character Heidi Abromowitz •118

45

The t is silent, as in Harlow.

Margot Asquith corrects Jean Harlow (and hints at her reputation) after the actress had mispronounced her first name; in T.S. Matthews, Great Tom (1973) •120

There, standing at the piano, was the original good time who had been had by all.

Kenneth Tynan, while an undergraduate, at an Oxford Union debate; (also attributed to Bette Davis of a passing starlet) •119

He proposed on a Valentine's day, although he didn't do it face to face, he did it in one of the little Valentine message bits in the paper. I think he had to pay for it by the word, because it just said 'Lee love Dawn, marriage?' which, you know I like, because it's not often you get something that's both romantic and thrifty.

Lucy Davis as Dawn in The Office, Series 1 Episode 4 •121

We have a BBC safety hazards form that we fill in before any production, but being kissed by Christine Hamilton didn't come into that unfortunately.

Louis Theroux, who made a documentary on disgraced Tory MP Neil Hamilton and his formidable wife. •122

A lot of men get very funny about women drinking: they don't really like it. Well, I'm sorry lads, but if we didn't get pissed, most of you would never get a shag.

Jenny Eclair •123

Steff: I've been out with a lot of girls at this school. I don't see what makes you so different.

Andie: I have some taste.

James Spader and Molly Ringwald in Pretty In Pink *(1986)* •124

I'll put an ad in the papers. Wanted, kind home for enormous savage rodent. Answers to the name of Sybil.

Long-suffering husband Basil Fawlty (John Cleese) looks to re-home his wife in **Fawlty Towers, 'Basil the Rat'** *1979* •125

Cher: I want to do something good for humanity.

Josh: Try sterilisation.

Alicia Silverstone and Paul Rudd in Clueless *(1995)* •126

Cordelia: You were too busy rushing off to die for your beloved Buffy… You'd never die for me.

Xander: I might die from you, does that get me any points?

Buffy the Vampire Slayer, 'Innocence' •127

You forget that the great British public would not care if Cuthbert Worsley had slept with mice.

Noél Coward; on refusing to allow his biographer Sheridan Morley to reveal his homosexuality, despite the recent 'outing' of theatre critic T.C. Worsley in Independent on Sunday *magazine, November 1995* •128

Believing that his hate
  for queers
Proclaimed his love
  for God,
He now (of all queer
  things, my dears)
Lies under his first sod.

Paul Dehn, on Sunday Express *editor John Gordon (1890-1974); in Nigel Rees,* **Cassell Dictionary of Humorous Quotations** *(1999)* •129

Marriage, n. The state or condition of a community consisting of a master, a mistress and two slaves, making in all, two.

Ambrose Bierce, The Devil's Dictionary *(1911)* •130

In Church your grandsire cut his throat;

To do the job too long he tarry'd,

He should have had my hearty vote,

To cut his throat before he marry'd.

Jonathan Swift, Verses On The Upright Judge *(1724)* •131

His ideal woman would be a stripper with a Budweiser in each hand.

Gwyneth Paltrow gets stuck in to her ex, Ben Affleck •132

I have always thought that every woman should marry, and no man.

Benjamin Disraeli •133

The trouble with some women is that they get all excited about nothing — and then they marry him.

Cher •134

Marriage makes an end of many short follies — being one long stupidity.

Friedrich Nietzsche •135

I'm sure Mick Jagger will find someone else to be unfaithful to soon. *Jerry Hall* •137

A TV host asked my wife, 'Have you ever considered divorce?' She replied: 'Divorce never, murder often.'

Charlton Heston; in Independent July 1999 •136

There was a time when those in public life attempted to behave with discretion and not like a stray mongrel in a public park.

Lord Cobham, whose wife left him for former Conservative Cabinet Minister David Mellor •138

Yes, he thinks
he's God Almighty.

*Lady Carina Fitzalan-Howard, on being
asked if her future husband David Frost
was religious; in* Sunday Times, *July 1985* •139

A man should
not insult his wife
publicly, at parties.
He should insult
her in the privacy
of the home.

James Thurber, from
Thurber Country
(1953) •140

Ye stupid auld bitch —
I beg your pardon, I
mistook ye for my wife.

*Lord Braxfield (1722-99) shouts at his whist
partner; attrib., quoted in* Literary Review,
November 2003 •141

Mrs Teasdale: My husband is dead.

Firefly: I'll bet he's just using that as an excuse.

Mrs Teasdale: I was with him to the end.

Firefly: No wonder he passed away.

Mrs Teasdale: I held him in my arms and kissed him.

Firefly: So it was murder!

Margaret Dumont and Groucho in Duck Soup *(1933)* •142

A man… is so in the way in the house!

Elizabeth Gaskell, Cranford *(1853)* •143

The comfortable estate of widowhood, is the only hope to keep up a wife's spirits.

John Gay, The Beggar's Opera *(1728)* •144

Admiral Roebuck (Geoffrey Palmer):
With all due respect M, I don't think
you have the balls for this.

M (Judi Dench):
Perhaps. The advantage is I don't have
to think with them all the time.

Exchange from **Tomorrow Never Dies** *(1997)* **with the woman
on top** *— a rare moment in a* **Bond** *movie.* •145

...Hell is other people.

Jean-Paul Sartre, Huis Clos, *(1944)* •146

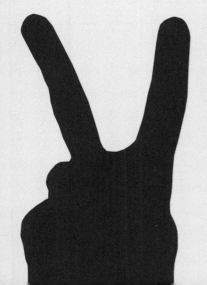

I have my bitchy side, but I don't think I'm really nasty. I think that a lot of other people probably think that I am. Fuck them.

Blondie front-woman Debbie Harry •147

I am very sorry to hear that Duff [Cooper] is surprised and grieved to hear that I had detested him for 23 years. I must have nicer manners than people normally credit me with.

Evelyn Waugh, letter to Lady Diana Cooper, 29 August 1953 •148

She proceeds to dip her little fountain-pen filler into pots of oily venom and to squirt this mixture at all her friends.

Harold Nicolson, of the society hostess Mrs Ronnie Greville; diary, 20 July 1937 •149

She really is very close to a charming character; if she had had the small pox she would have been so.

Mrs Gaskell on Effie Gray, John Ruskin's wife •150

I cannot compassionate the countess, since I think her insolent character deserves all the mortifications Heaven can send her.

Lady Mary Wortley Montagu •151

Neighbours. I'd rather have thrush.
Pamela Stephenson •152

I have got several very bad
new lunatics, most of them
religious, and some just
ordinary housewives,
who try to write a little.
*Edith Sitwell on the guests at a forthcoming
dinner party at her house* •153

I must go and see what that poor
gaping imbecile my charwoman
is doing about dinner.
Virginia Woolf •154

Dinner at the Hunterscombes'
possessed 'only two dramatic
features — the wine was a
farce and the food a tragedy'.
Anthony Powell, The Acceptance World
(1955) •155

When he has a party, you not
only bring your own scotch, you
bring your own rocks.
George Burns on Jack Benny •156

Very sorry can't come.
Lie follows by post.
*Baron Beresford replying to an invitation
to dinner from Edward Prince of Wales* •157

I've had a perfectly wonderful
evening, but this wasn't it.
Groucho Marx •158

Bore, n. A person who talks when you wish him to listen.

Ambrose Bierce •159

At a party one evening the painter James McNeill Whistler found himself cornered by a notorious bore. "You know, Mr Whistler," the bore said, "I passed your house last night." "Thank you", Whistler replied.

Whistler •160

He is not only dull in himself, but the cause of dullness in others.

Samuel Foote, on a dull lord, in Boswell's Life of Samuel Johnson *(1791)* 1783 •161

Underneath this flabby exterior is an enormous lack of character.

Oscar Levant,
Memoirs of an Amnesiac
(1965) •162

I've tried him drunk and I've tried him sober but there's nothing in him.

Charles II (1630-85), of his niece Anne's husband George of Denmark, in Guila Curtis, The Life and Times of Queen Anne *(1972)* •163

Champagne for my real friends, and real pain for my sham friends.

Francis Bacon (1909-92) makes his favourite toast; Michael Peppiatt, **Francis Bacon** *(1996)* •164

A Merry Christmas to all my friends except two.

W.C. Fields, attrib. •165

You and I were long friends;
you are now my enemy,
and I am
Yours,
B. Franklin

> *Benjamin Franklin,* **letter to William Strahan** •166

Cicely: When I see a spade, I call it a spade.
Gwendolen: I am glad to say that I have never seen a spade. It is obvious that our social spheres have been widely different.

Oscar Wilde, *The Importance of* **Being Earnest** *(1895) Act III* •167

The truckman, the trashman and the policeman on the block may call me Alice but you may not.

Alice Roosevelt Longworth to Senator *Joseph McCarthy; in Michael Teague,* **Mrs L: Conversations with Alice Roosevelt** **Longworth** *(1981)* •169

Grandmother used to take my mother to the circus to see the fat lady and tattooed man. Now they're everywhere.

Joan Collins •168

He was like a cock who thought the sun had risen to hear him crow.

George Eliot, **Adam Bede,** *(1859)* •171

Egotism — usually just a case of mistaken nonentity.

Barbara Stanwyck, American actress. •170

Blessed are the famous, for they will enjoy the praise of men.

The Archbishop of Canterbury satirises modern values •172

Repartee, n.
Prudent insult in retort. Practiced by gentlemen with a constitutional aversion to violence, but a strong disposition to offend. *Ambrose Bierce,*
The Devil's Dictionary
(1911) •173

You can file Madonna's quote in the dictionary of clichés under 'pot and kettle'.
Ben Affleck responds to Madonna's reported accusation that he and Jennifer Lopez had courted media attention •174

You can't shame or humiliate modern celebrities. What used to be called shame and humiliation is now called publicity. And forgot traditional character assassination. If you say a modern celebrity is an adulterer, a pervert, and a drug addict, all it means is you've read his autobiography.
P.J. O'Rourke, **The Enemies List,** *1996* •175

Television is an invention that permits you to be entertained in your living room by people you wouldn't have in your home.
David Frost •176

We invite people like that to tea, but we don't marry them.

Lady Chetwode on her future son-in-law, John Betjeman •177

There is very little pure blood left in this country, as most of it is tainted with cocaine.

Jenny Eclair on the English upper classes •179

I can't see the sense in it really. It makes me a Commander of the British Empire. They might as well make me a Commander of Milton Keynes — at least that exists.

Spike Milligan on the 'honour' of being made a CBE in 1992; attrib., **Daily Telegraph** *February 2002* •178

He's the sort of person who, two hundred years ago would have died leading a cavalry charge into a volcano.

Frankie Boyle on Boris Johnson
Mock the Week •180

The institution of monarchy is inherently silly.

Lord Hattersley •181

Henry VIII, or King Syphilis Gut Bucket Wife Murderer VIII as I prefer to call him, was born in 1491. *Jo Brand* •182

Eulogy, n. Praise of a person who has either the advantages of wealth and power, or the consideration to be dead.

Ambrose Bierce, **The Devil's Dictionary** *(1911)* •183

Here lies a great and mighty king
Whose promise none relies on;
He never said a foolish thing
Nor ever did a wise one.

John Wilmot, Earl of Rochester composes **'The King's Epitaph** *for reigning monarch Charles II* •184

This is very true: for my words are my own, and my actions are my ministers'.

Charles II's response to Rochester's epitaph; in Thomas Hearne: **Remarks and Collections** *(1885-1921)* •185

Who's your fat friend?

George 'Beau' Brummel, to Beau Nash as the latter appeared accompanied by the Prince Regent, later George IV •186

Most Gracious Queen,
  we thee implore

To go away and sin no more,

But if that effort be too great,

To go away at any rate.

Anonymous; epigram on Queen Caroline (Caroline of Brunswick), unpopular wife of George IV, quoted in a letter from Francis Burton to Lord Colchester, *November 1820* •188

A more contemptible, cowardly, selfish, unfeeling dog does not exist than this King… with vices and weakness of the lowest and most contemptible order.

Charles Greville, diarist, on George IV •187

The King blew his nose twice, and wiped the royal perspiration repeatedly from a face which is probably the largest uncivilised spot in England.

Oliver Wendell Holmes on British monarch William IV •189

For seventeen years George V did nothing at all but kill animals and stick in stamps.

Harold Nicolson •190

It's most unfortunate that all my sons have such long eyelashes while my daughter hasn't any at all.

The Queen on Princess Anne (and co.) •191

Such an attractive lass. So outdoorsy. She loves nature in spite of what it did to her.

Bette Midler on Princess Anne •192

Of all the Royals, Anne is the rudest. If anyone crosses her, she lays back her ears, bares her teeth, and kicks them to splinters.

Jean Rook •193

She is a lady short on looks, absolutely deprived of any dress sense, has a figure like a Jurassic monster (seems) very greedy when it comes to loot, lacks tact and wants to upstage everyone else.

Sir Nicholas Fairbairn on Sarah, the Duchess of York, in the Independent. •194

Shea was a master of evasion, more slippery than a Jacuzzi full of KY Jelly.

Richard Littlejohn on Michael Shea, the Queen's former press secretary, in The Sun •196

I couldn't believe it when I picked up a newspaper and read that 82 per cent of men would rather sleep with a goat than me.

Sarah Ferguson •195

If one were going to be interviewed by anyone, it wouldn't be you.

The Queen shows John Humphrys of Radio 4's Today *programme that she too has mastered that art of the put-down* •197

Prince Charles is an insensitive, hypocritical oaf and Princess Diana is a selfish, empty-headed bimbo. They should never have got married in the first place. I blame the parents.

Richard Littlejohn, in The Sun •198

I cannot but conclude the bulk of your natives to be the most pernicious race of little odious vermin that nature ever suffered to crawl upon the surface of the earth.

Jonathan Swift, Gulliver's Travels *(1726)* 'A Voyage to Brobdingnag' •199

America is the only nation in history which miraculously has gone directly from barbarism to degeneration without the usual interval of civilisation.

Georges Clemenceau •200

Why cannot you go down to Bristol and see some of the third and fourth class people there, and they'll do just as well?

Lady Holland to Charles Dickens, on hearing of his proposed trip to America; in U. Pope-Hennessy, Charles Dickens *(1947)* •201

Their demeanour… is invariably morose, sullen, clownish, and repulsive. I should think there is not, on the face of the earth, a people so entirely destitute of humour, vivacity, or the capacity of enjoyment.

Charles Dickens is decidedly unimpressed by the American people •202

The only real native of Kansas is the buffalo. He's got a very hard head, a very uncertain temper, and a very lonely future. Apart from that, there's hardly any comparison between you.

Errol Flynn as Wade Hatton to Olivia De Havilland in Dodge City •203

> A big hard-boiled city with no more personality than a paper cup.

Raymond Chandler on LA,
The Little Sister, *1949* •204

How DOES America live with itself? Just by FORGETTING itself? Like an incontinent old man: stinks but ain't sure WHY. *American novelist Lucy Ellmann* •206

New York makes one think of the collapse of civilisation, about Sodom and Gomorrah, the end of the world. The end wouldn't come as a surprise here. Many people already bank on it.
Saul Bellow, **Mr Sammler's Planet** *(1970)* •205

In Australia,
Inter alia,
Mediocrities
Think they're Socrates.

Peter Porter, unpublished clerihew;
in Stephen Murray-Smith (ed.),
The Dictionary of Australian
Quotations *(1984)* •207

And what has China
ever given the world?
Can you really respect
a nation that's never
taken to cutlery?

Victoria Wood •208

Afrikaans sounds like
Welsh with attitude
and emphysema.

A.A. Gill •209

To speak with your mouth full
And swallow with greed
Are national traits
Of the travelling Swede.

Duff Cooper; in Philip Ziegler,
Diana Cooper *(1981)* •210

71

The best that can be said
for Norweigan television
is that it gives you the
sensation of a coma without
the worry and inconvenience.
Bill Bryson, **Neither Here Nor There**
(1991) •211

I don't like Norwegians at all.
The sun never sets, the bar
never opens, and the whole
country smells of kippers.

Evelyn Waugh, **letter to Lady Diana
Cooper,** *13 July 1934* •212

In Italy for thirty years under the
Borgias they had warfare, terror,
murder, bloodshed — they produced
Michelangelo, Leonardo da Vinci and
the Renaissance. In Switzerland they
had brotherly love, five hundred years
of democracy and peace and what
did they produce…? The cuckoo clock.
Orson Welles, **The Third Man** *(1949 film);
Welles added these lines to Graham
Greene's script* •213

I look upon Switzerland
as an inferior sort of
Scotland. *Sydney Smith,* **letter to
Lord Holland,** *1815* •214

Frogs… are slightly better
than Huns or Wops, but
abroad is unutterably bloody
and foreigners are fiends.

*A little bit of xenophobia from Nancy
Mitford,* **The Pursuit of Love** *(1945)* •215

Every wise and thoroughly
worldy wench

Knows there's always something
fishy about the French!

Noël Coward, 'There's Always Something
Fishy About the French' •217

Let's be frank, the
Italians' technological
contribution to
humankind stopped
with the pizza oven.

Bill Bryson, Neither Here Nor There *(1991)* •216

I hate the French,
I hate them all
From Toulouse Lafucking Trec
to Charles de Gaulle.

Paul Scott Goodman, 'I Hate the French'
(from the musical Bright Lights, Big City,
1988, after the book by Jay McInerney) •218

He took offence at my description of Edinburgh as the Reykjavik of the South.

Tom Stoppard, **Jumpers** *(1972)* •219

I hate you English. With your boring trousers and your shiny toilet paper and your ridiculous preconceptions that Frenchmen are great lovers. I'm French and I'm hung like a baby carrot and a couple of petit pois.

Chris Barrie as the Ambassador in **Blackadder the Third,** 'Nob and Nobility', *1987* •221

The land of my fathers. My fathers can have it.

Dylan Thomas of his Welsh homeland, **Adam** *December 1953* •220

The English are, I think the most obtuse and barbarous people in the world.
Stendhal *(Marie Henri Beyle)* •222

For 'tis a low, newspaper, humdrum, lawsuit, Country.
Lord Byron, of England, **Don Juan** *(1819-24)* •223

I've noticed that the English are not given to it.
Gore Vidal, on the suggestion that, in his books, washing has some symbolic significance; attrib., in The Guardian *February 1999* •224

An Englishman thinks he is moral when he is only uncomfortable.
George Bernard Shaw, **Man and Superman** *(1903)* •225

"There is nothing good to be had in the country, or if there is, they will not let you have it.

William Hazlitt,
The Round Table *(1817)* •226

One has no great hopes for Birmingham. I always say there is something direful in the sound.

Mrs Elton in Jane Austen's **Emma** *(1816)* •227

Come, friendly bombs, and fall on Slough! It isn't fit for humans now.

John Betjeman, 'Slough' *(1937)* •228

I would like to live in Manchester, England. The transition between Manchester and death would be unnoticeable.

Mark Twain •229

Immigrant, n.
An unenlightened person who thinks
one country better than another.
Ambrose Bierce, The Devil's Dictionary *(1911)* •230

…when political ammunition runs low, inevitably the rusty artillery of abuse is always wheeled into action.

Adlai Stevenson, speech, 1952 •231

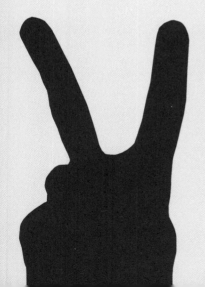

> He was a man of splendid abilities but utterly corrupt. Like rotten mackerel by moonlight, he shines and stinks.

John Randolph (1773-1833), member of the House of Representatives for Roanoak, Virginia, on jurist and statesman Edward Livingstone •232

Alexander Smith:
  You, sir, speak for the present generation, but I speak for posterity.
Henry Clay:
  Yes, and you seem resolved to speak until the arrival of your audience.

Henry Clay, in the U.S. Senate; Robert V. Remini, Henry Clay *(1991)* •233

John Randolph:
  I never sidestep skunks.
Henry Clay:
  I always do.

American politician Henry Clay unexpectedly moved out of the way of his political rival John Randolph of Roanoke; in Robert V. Remini, Henry Clay *(1991)* •234

He has all the characteristics of a dog except loyalty.

Texan hero Sam 'The Raven' Houston on fellow soldier and legislator Thomas Jefferson Green •235

Even wisdom from him seems but folly.

The New York Post *take an unsympathetic view of Abraham Lincoln* •236

…We did not conceive it possible that even Mr Lincoln would produce a paper so slipshod, so loose-joined, so puerile, not alone in literary construction but in its ideas, its sentiments, its grasp. He has outdone himself. He has literally come out of the little end of his own horn. By the side of it, mediocrity is superb.

A contemporary review of Lincoln's Gettysburg Address from the **Chicago Times,** *1863* •237

They never open their mouths without subtracting from the sum of human knowledge.

Thomas Reed (1839-1902), Speaker of the US House of Representatives, on members of Congress •238

Heckler: I'm a Democrat!

Theodore *Roosevelt:* May I ask the gentleman why he is a Democrat?

Heckler: My grandfather was a Democrat; my father was a Democrat; and I am a Democrat.

Roosevelt: My friend, suppose your grandfather had been a jackass and your father was a jackass, what would you be?

Heckler (without hesitation): A Republican!

Theodore Roosevelt grapples with a heckler and loses •239

He has no more backbone than a chocolate éclair.

Theodore Roosevelt on
William E. McKinley •240

My father always wanted to be the corpse at every funeral, the bride at every wedding and the baby at every christening.

Alice Roosevelt Longworth, on
President Theodore Roosevelt,
quoted in Celebrity Register,
1963 •241

One always thinks of him as a glorified bouncer engaged eternally in cleaning out bar-rooms — and not too proud to gouge when the inspiration came to him, or to bite in the clinches.

H.L. Mencken on Theodore Roosevelt,
Prejudices, Second Series, *(1920)* •242

He writes the worst English that I have ever encountered. It reminds me of a string of wet sponges; it reminds me of tattered washing on the line; it reminds me of stale bean soup, of college yells, or dogs barking idiotically through endless nights.

H.L. Mencken, on US President Warren G. Harding, Baltimore Evening Sun, *1921* •243

His speeches left the impression of an army of pompous phrases moving over the landscape in search of an idea.

William G. McAdoo, Democratic, on Warren G. Harding •244

He looks as if he had been weaned on a pickle.

Alice Roosevelt Longworth, on Calvin Coolidge. •245

Following Eleanor Roosevelt in search of irrationality is like following a burning fuse in search of an explosive; one never has to wait very long.

William F Buckley jr. •246

Never underestimate a man who overestimates himself.
Franklin D. Roosevelt, on General Douglas MacArthur •247

One third Eleanor and two-thirds mush.

Alice Roosevelt Longworth (daughter of President Teddy), on Franklin D. Roosevelt •248

My choice early in life was either to be a piano-player in a whorehouse or a politician. And to tell the truth, there's hardly any difference.

Harry S. Truman, 1962 •249

A triumph for democracy. It proves that a millionaire has just as good a chance as anybody else.

Bob Hope, on John F. Kennedy's electoral victory in Wisconsin; on a 1960 TV programme, recalled in **William Robert Faith**, Bob Hope *(1983)* •250

Not unlike Hitler, but without the charm.

Gore Vidal on conservative journalist Willam F. Buckley Jr, who he'd dubbed a 'crypto-Nazi' during a televised debate in 1968 •252

Reading a speech with his usual sense of discovery.

Gore Vidal, of former-President Eisenhower at the Republican convention of 1964 •251

Now listen, you queer, stop calling me a crypto-Nazi or I'll sock you in your goddamn face, and you'll stay plastered.

Buckley's response to the crypto-Nazi comment. •253

85

He is the kind of politician who would cut down a redwood tree and then mount the stump to make a speech for conservation.
Adlai Stevenson on Nixon •254

I may not know much, but I know chicken shit from a chicken salad.

Lyndon Baines Johnson, on a speech by Richard Nixon; Merle Miller, Lyndon *(1980)* •255

He can lie out of both sides of his mouth at the same time, and if he ever caught himself telling the truth, he'd lie just to keep his hand in.

Harry Truman on Richard Nixon •256

Nixon's motto, if two wrongs don't make a right, try three.
Laurence J. Peter •257

A group of politicians deciding to dump a President because his morals are bad is like the Mafia getting together to bump off the Godfather for not going to church on Sunday.

Russell Baker on Nixon and the Watergate scandal, The New York Times, *1974.* •258

Richard Nixon impeached himself. He gave us Gerald Ford as his revenge.

Bella Abzug in **Rolling Stone;** *in* **Linda Botts, Loose Talk** *(1980)* •259

He looks like the guy in a science fiction movie who is the first to see the Creature.

David Frye on Gerald Ford •260

So dumb he can't fart and chew gum at the same time.

Lyndon Baines Johnson, of Gerald Ford, in Richard Reeves, **A Ford, not a Lincoln** *(1975)* •261

> A triumph of the embalmer's art.

Gore Vidal, of Ronald Reagan; in Observer, *26 April 1981* •262

I believe that Ronald Reagan can make this country what it once was — an Arctic region covered with ice.

Steve Martin •263

People here may be sharply divided over the Reagan administration's politics — but they admire Ronald Reagan for not getting involved in them.

Edward Kennedy, Democrat Senator •264

The battle for the mind of Ronald Reagan was like the trench warfare of World War I. Never have so many fought so hard for such barren terrain.

Peggy Noonan; What I Saw at the Revolution *(1990)* •265

A senescent bimbo with a lust for home furnishings.

Barbara Ehrenreich on Nancy Reagan •266

Washington couldn't tell a lie, Nixon couldn't tell the truth and Reagan couldn't tell the difference.

Mort Sahl, American comedian. •267

Poor George, he can't help it — he was born with a silver foot in his mouth.

Former Texas governor Ann Richards, of George Bush Snr., in a keynote speech at the Democratic convention; in Independent, *July 1988* •268

An empty suit that goes to funerals and plays golf.

Ross Perot on Vice President Dan Quayle •269

Unlike the current occupant of the White House, he has no difficulty in orally extemporising a series of grammatical English sentences, each containing a main verb.

Boris Johnson, with an unlikely (and probably insincere) endorsement of Barack Obama •270

Political pundits are saying President George W. Bush has made gains in two key states: dazed and confused

David Letterman •271

Both candidates now are trying to lower expectations for how they'll do on the debates. For example, Kerry tried to lower expectations for himself by saying Bush has never lost a debate and that he is a formidable opponent. Then Bush lowered expectations for himself when he said, 'Hey, what does formidable mean?

Jay Leno, on the televised debates between Bush and Sen. John Kerry in the run-up to the 2004 presidential election •272

The president finally explained why he sat in that classroom on 9/11 for 7 minutes after he was told the country was under attack. He said he was 'collecting his thoughts.' What a time to start a new hobby.
Bill Maher •273

She looks like some sulphurous video vicar, who, any day now, will be found in a motel somewhere, under a heap of prostitutes.

Martin Amis' on a picture of Hillary Clinton used on a book dust jacket •274

I would like to apologize for referring to George W. Bush as a 'deserter.' What I meant to say is that George W. Bush is a deserter, an election thief, a drunk driver, a WMD liar, and a functional illiterate. And he poops his pants.
Michael Moore •275

No one ever went broke underestimating the taste of the great American public.
H.L. Mencken •276

There they are, a conga line of suckholes on the Conservative side of Australian politics. The backbench sucks up to the Prime Minister and the prime minister sucks up to George W.

Former Australian Labour PM Paul Keating launches an attack on John Howard, then Liberal PM, for co-operation with the US on Iraq •277

If it's a boy, I'll call it after myself. If it's a girl, I'll call it Victoria, after our Queen. But if, as I strongly suspect, it's nothing but piss and wind, I'll call it after you.

Australian PM Sir George Reid, on being asked by journalists what he was going to christen his corpulent stomach •278

This little flower, this delicate little beauty, this cream puff, is supposed to be beyond personal criticism… He is simply a shiver looking for a spine to run up.

Paul Keating, of Australian Liberal leader John Hewson; in **Ned Sherrin in his Anecdotage** *(1993); Harold Wilson is also said to have called Ted Heath 'a shiver looking for a spine to run up'* •279

Like being flogged with a warm lettuce.

Australian Prime Minister Paul Keating, referring to an attack by the opposition leader, John Hewson •280

For socialists, going to bed with the Liberals is like having oral sex with a shark.

Larry Zolf comments on the Canadian political scene, 1975 •281

93

Boswell: So, Sir, you laugh at schemes of
   political improvement.
Johnson: Why, Sir, most schemes of political
   improvement are very laughable things.

Samuel Johnson; in James Boswell, Life of Samuel Johnson *(1791)*
26 October 1769 •282

Mrs Miggins: You better watch out, Mr Blackadder.
   Things are bound to change.
Blackadder: Not while Pitt the Elder's Prime Minister. He's
   about as effective as a cat flap in an elephant house. And
   as long as his feet are warm and he gets a cup of nice milky
   tea in the sun before his morning nap, he doesn't bother
   anyone until his potty needs emptying.

Blackadder the Third, 'Dish and Dishonety', *1987* •283

Earl of Sandwich: 'Pon my soul, Wilkes, I don't know whether you'll die upon the gallows or of the pox.

Wilkes: That depends, my Lord, on whether I embrace your Lordship's principles, or your Lordship's mistress.

John Wilkes; in Sir Charles Petrie, The Four Georges (1935); probably apocryphal •284

Richard Brinsley Sheridan's son Tom declared that when he became an MP, he would proclaim his independence of party by emblazoning his forehead with the words 'To Let'. His father replied: 'And, under that, Tom, write 'unfurnished'.

Richard Brinsley Sheridan; Walter Jerrold, Bon-Mots (1893) •285

The Right Honourable Gentleman is indebted to his memory for his jests and to his imagination for his facts.

Playwright and MP Richard Brinsley Sheridan (1751-1816), on the Earl of Dundad •286

He is a self-made man, and worships his creator.

Conservative MP Benjamin Disraeli on Liberal statesman and radical Corn Law activist John Bright. •287

The Right Honourable Gentleman is reminiscent of a poker. The only difference is that a poker gives off occasional signs of warmth.

British Conservative politician Benjamin Disraeli (1804-1881), of former Conservative Prime Minister Sir Robert Peel •288

The ministers [on the Treasury Bench] reminded me of one of those marine landscapes not very uncommon on the coast of South America. You behold a range of exhausted volcanoes. Not a flame flickers on a single pallid crest.

Benjamin Disraeli, speech at Manchester, April 1872 •289

He has not a single redeeming defect.

Benjamin Disraeli on W.E. Gladstone •290

He made his conscience not his guide but his accomplice.

Benjamin Disraeli on W.E. Gladstone •291

A sophisticated rhetorician, inebriated with the exhuberance of his own verbosity.

Benjamin Disraeli parodies Gladstone's high-falutin' style; in The Times, *July 1878* •292

If Gladstone fell into the Thames, that would be a misfortune, and if anybody pulled him out that, I suppose, would be a calamity.

Benjamin Disraeli, on being asked to distinguish between a misfortune and a calamity: •293

His impact on history would be no more than the whiff of scent on a lady's purse.

David Lloyd George, on Arthur Balfour, British PM 1902-1905 •294

He might make an adequate Lord Mayor of Birmingham in a lean year.

David Lloyd George on Neville Chamberlain; in Leon Harris, **The Fine Art of Political Wit** *(1965)* •295

A very weak-minded fellow I am afraid, and, like the feather pillow, bears the marks of the last person who has sat on him!

British army commander Earl Haig describes the 17th Earl of Derby; in a letter to Lady Haig, 1918. (Often mistakenly attrib. to Lloyd George.) •296

He was brilliant to the top of his army boots.

David Lloyd George on General Haig •297

My vigour, vitality and cheek repel me. I am the kind of woman I would run away from.

Nancy Astor, British politician. •298

The worst thing I can say about democracy is that it has tolerated the Right Honourable Gentleman [Neville Chamberlain] for four and a half years.

Aneurin ('Nye') Bevan, speech in the House of Commons 23 July 1929 •299

Listening to a speech by Chamberlain is like paying a visit to Woolworth's: everything in its place and nothing above sixpence.

British Labour politician Aneurin Bevan (1897-1960), on Conservative MP and Prime Minister Neville Chamberlain. •300

The Right Honourable and Learned Gentleman has twice crossed the floor of this House, each time leaving behind a trail of slime.

David Lloyd George on Sir John Simon •301

His fame endures; we shall not forget The name of Baldwin until we're out of debt.

Kensal Green on Conservative politician and Prime Minister Stanley Baldwin (PM 1923-4 1924-9, 1935-7) •302

Of course I believe in the Devil. How else would I account for the existence of Lord Beaverbrook?

Evelyn Waugh, of British newspaper proprietor and Conservative politician Max Aitken, 1st Baron Beaverbrook; in L. Gourlay, The Beaverbrook I Knew *(1984)* •303

I remember, when I was a child, being taken to the celebrated Barnum's circus, which contained an exhibition of freaks and monstrosities; but the exhibit on the programme which I most desired to see was the one described as 'The Boneless Wonder'. My parents judged that the spectacle would be too revolting and demoralising for my youthful eyes, and I have waited fifty years to see 'The Boneless Wonder' sitting on the Treasury Bench.

Winston Churchill, of Labour politician Ramsay MacDonald; speech recorded in Hansard, *28 January 1931* •304

[Churchill] would make a drum out of the skin of his mother in order to sound his own praises.

David Lloyd George; in Paul Johnson (ed.), The Oxford Book of Political Anecdotes (1986); a similar comment about Churchill is attributed to Margot Asquith •305

Bessie Braddock, MP: Winston, you're drunk! *Churchill:* Bessie, you're ugly. But tomorrow I shall be sober.

A legendary exchange allegedly between Bessie Braddock and Winston Churchill, although versions exist attributing this witticism to George Bernard Shaw •306

Mr Gladstone read Homer for fun, which I thought served him right.
Churchill •307

If you wanted nothing done, Arthur Balfour was the best man for the task. There was no equal to him.

Churchill on Arthur Balfour (Conservative politician, and Prime Minister 1902-6) •308

In the depths of that dusty soul there is nothing but abject surrender.
Churchill on Chamberlain •309

We know that he has, more than any other man, the gift of compressing the largest amount of words into smallest amount of thought.

Winston Churchill on Ramsay Macdonald,1933 •310

Who is this man whose name is neither one thing nor the other?

Winston Churchill, of MP and prominent architect Alfred Bossom; attrib. •311

He occasionally stumbled over the truth, but hastily picked himself up and hurried on as if nothing had happened.

Winston Churchill, of British Conservative politician Stanley Baldwin; in J.L. Lane (ed.), The Sayings of Winston Churchill *(1992)* •312

The only recorded instance in history of a rat swimming towards a sinking ship.

Winston Churchill, of a former Conservative who proposed to defect to the Liberals; Leon Harris, The Fine Art of Political Wit *(1965)* •313

What can you do with a man who looks like a female llama surprised when bathing?

Winston Churchill on Charles de Gaulle; in conversation, c.1944; David Fraser Alanbrooke *(1982)* •314

I sympathize with General von Thoma. Defeated, humiliated, in captivity, and… (long pause for dramatic effect)… dinner with Montgomery.

Churchill, after Monty controversially invited a captive German General to dine with him •315

In defeat, unbeatable; in victory, unbearable.

Churchill on Montgomery •316

[Clement Attlee] is a modest man who has a great deal to be modest about.

Winston Churchill on Clement Attlee, Labour politician and his successor as Prime Minister in 1945; in Chicago Sunday Tribune Magazine of Books *June 1954* •317

A sheep in sheep's clothing.

Winston Churchill on Clement Attlee; in Lord Home, The Way the Wind Blows *(1976)* •318

They are not fit to manage a whelk stall.

Churchill on the Labour Party in 1945 •319

He has all the virtues I dislike and none of the vices I admire.

Churchill on Stafford Cripps •320

A merchant of discourtesy.

Churchill on Nye Bevan •321

I welcome this opportunity of pricking the bloated bladder of lies with the poniard of truth.

Aneurin Bevan on Winston Churchill •322

If you recognize anyone, it does not mean that you like him. We all, for instance, recognize the honourable Member of the Ebbw Vale.

Churchill uses Britain's recognition of Communist China to have a pop at his old adversary, Nye Bevan •323

He is a man suffering from petrified adolescence.

Nye Bevan on Churchill •324

Winston had devoted the best years of his life to preparing his impromptu speeches.

F.E.Smith on Churchill •325

> I am not going to spend any time whatsoever in attacking the foreign secretary. Quite honestly I am beginning to feel quite sorry for him. If we complain about the truth, there is no reason to attack the monkey when the organ grinder is present.

Aneurin Bevan, preferring to enter into debate with PM Churchill than Foreign Secretary Eden •326

Lord Birkenhead is very clever but sometimes his brains go to his head.
Margot Asquith on Conservative politician and lawyer F.E. Smith, 1st Earl of Birkenhead; in Listener *11 June 1953,* **'Margot Oxford' by Lady Violet Bonham Carter** •327

An overripe banana, yellow outside, squishy in.

Sir Reginald Paget on Anthony Eden •328

He enjoys prophesying the imminent fall of the capitalist system and is prepared to play a part, any part, in its burial — except that of a mute.
Conservative politician and Prime Minister Harold Macmillan, on the perpetually vocal Nye Bevan •329

That's the trouble with Anthony — half mad baronet, half beautiful woman.

R.A. Butler, of British Conservative politician and Prime Minister Anthony Eden; attrib. •330

He was not only a bore; he bored for England.

Malcolm Muggeridge of Anthony Eden; Tread Softly *(1966)* •331

If Harold Wilson ever went to school without any boots, it was merely because he was too big for them.

Harold Macmillan casts aspersions on Harold Wilson's claims of a poor upbringing •332

Dull Alec versus Smart Alec.

David Frost compares Alec Douglas-Home and Harold Wilson; in That Was The Week That Was, *1963* •333

Randolph Churchill went into hospital… to have a lung removed. It was announced that the trouble was not 'malignant'… It was a typical triumph of modern science to find the only part of Randolph that was not malignant and remove it.

Evelyn Waugh on Winston's son; 'Irregular Notes 1960-65'; diary *March 1964* •334

I do not often attack the Labour Party. They do it so well themselves.
Edward Heath, speech, 1973 •335

Tory MP John Blackburn: Mr Speaker, I am very disappointed in you.

George Thomas, Speaker of the House of Commons: Why is that, John?

Blackburn: Well, Mr Speaker, you have denied the House the opportunity to hear a brilliant speech on this subject. I have in my pocket here a splendid speech and by not calling me you have denied the House the opportunity to hear this, the best speech I have ever prepared.

Thomas: It's always the same with you, John, isn't it?

Blackburn: What do you mean, Mr Speaker?

Thomas: Whenever I don't call you, you have prepared the most brilliant speech of all time, yet whenever I do call you, you deliver a fucking awful one.

Parliamentary exchange, as told by Blackburn himself •336

He represents what I despise the most — sanctimony, guile, slime and intrigue under a cloak of decency, all for self-advancement — it's called hypocrisy.

Presumably the subject, Willie Whitelaw, had offended Nicholas Fairbairn •337

The Labour Party is going around stirring up apathy.

William Whitelaw; recalled by Alan Watkins as a characteristic 'Willieism'; in Observer, *May 1983 •338*

Child: Mamma, are Tories born wicked, or do they grow wicked afterwards?
Mother: They are born wicked, and grow worse.

Anonymous, in G.W.E. Russell, **Collections and Recollections** *(1898)* •339

The reason that there are so few female politicians is that it is too much trouble to put make-up on two faces.

Maureen Murphy •340

Attila the Hen.

Clement Freud on Margaret Thatcher •341

She sounded like the Book of Revelations read out over a railway station public address system by a headmistress of a certain age wearing calico knickers.

Clive James of Margaret Thatcher (on television, quoted in **Observer***, 1979)* •342

I cannot bring myself to vote for a woman who has been voice-trained to speak to me as though my dog had just died.

Keith Waterhouse, English humorist, on Margaret Thatcher •343

Margaret Thatcher says she has given the French President a piece of her mind — this is not a gift I would receive with alacrity.

Denis Healey •344

She is a petty-minded xenophobe who struts around the world interfering and lecturing in an arrogant and high-handed manner.
Tony Banks on Thatcher •345

She is about as environmentally friendly as the bubonic plague.
Tony Banks on Thatcher •346

A Prime Minister whose self-righteous stubbornness has not been equalled, save briefly by Neville Chamberlain, since Lord North.
Roy Jenkins, of Margaret Thatcher, in Observer *March 1990* •347

When she speaks without thinking she says what she thinks.
Norman St John Stevas on Margaret Thatcher •348

She measured the price of everything and the value of nothing.
Tony Benn's scathing summary of Margaret Thatcher's time in office •349

In the blue corner, Edwina Currie, who remains ineluctably Edwina Currie… One third evil fairytale queen, one third vampiric bat and one third Spitting Image puppet.

Lucy Mangan, Guardian TGV columnist on Come Dine With Me Election Special, May 2010 – Part 1 •350

In the red corner, Derek Hatton, the Trotskyite former Liverpool councillor turned — God help us all — motivational speaker, although he couldn't motivate me to get out of a burning car.

Lucy Mangan, Guardian TGV columnist on Come Dine With Me Election Special, May 2010 – Part 2 •351

Might as well have a corncob up his arse.

Alan Clark MP, on Douglas Hurd MP •352

When he leaves the chamber, he probably goes to vandalise a few paintings somewhere. He is to the arts what Vlad the Impaler was to origami… He is undoubtedly living proof that a pig's bladder on a stick can be elected as a member of parliament.

Tony Banks on Tory MP Terry Dicks after the latter opposed state funding for the arts •353

He is in government principally because of his ability to give a good news gloss to any disaster that turns up. He is a man who would have hailed the sinking of the Titanic as a first in underwater exploration. He would have greeted the Black Death as a necessary step towards a leaner and fitter economy. He would have celebrated the Great Fire of London as a vital contribution to urban regeneration.

Bryan Gould on David Mellor •354

Neil Kinnock's speeches go on for so long because he has nothing to say, so he has no way of knowing when he's finished saying it.

John Major •355

He is so ambitious
that he squeaks
when he walks, and
cannot manage to
smile at any colleague
inferior in rank in
case he compromises
himself in some way.

Alan Clark, of Conservative Education
Secretary John Patten, in Diaries — into
Politics, *(2000)* •356

He has been described by John
Major as the minister for little
people — he seems more like
the minister for paperclips to me.

John Prescott on William Waldegrave's
appointment as the Secretary of State for
John Major's Citizens Charter •357

When I hear the name Richard Body I hear the sound of white coats flapping.

John Major, on one of his own MP's, 1994. attrib. •358

At least it wasn't Ann Widdecombe.

Pat Dessoy, John Major's sister, on revelations about Major's 1980s affair with Edwina Currie •359

Is there no beginning to your talents?

Clive Anderson to Jeffrey Archer •360

He has something of the night about him.

Tory MP Ann Widdecombe, on her former boss and Home Secretary Michael Howard, 1997 •361

Hacker: Humphrey, do you see it as part of your job to help ministers make fools of themselves?

Sir Humphrey: Well, I never met one that needed any help.

Paul Eddington *and* Nigel Hawthorne *in* Yes, Minister, 'The Right to Know' (written by Antony Jay & Jonathan Lynn), *1980* •362

Ecological activist: There is nothing special about man, Mr. Hacker. We're not above nature. We're all part of it. Men are animals too, you know.

Hacker: I know that — I've just come from the House of Commons!

Yes, Minister, 'The Right to Know' (written by Antony Jay & Jonathan Lynn), *1980* •363

Peter Mandelson is a sweet guy, you know. But I eat lots of garlic and I sleep with garlic flowers round my neck. So I'm safe… for the moment.
Tony Banks on Peter Mandelson, May 1998 •364

Peter Mandelson is someone who can skulk in broad daylight.
Simon Hoggart, in **The Guardian** *July 1998* •365

The effect is of a Womble taking Cerberus for a walk.

Will Cohn, of British Labour politician (and now life peer) Roy Hattersley and his dog Buster; in **Daily Telegraph** *September 1998* •366

John Prescott has the face of a man who clubs baby seals to death.

Denis Healey •367

I was very relieved when the child was born at the Chelsea and Westminster hospital. I had thought he would be born in a manger.
Leo Abse on the birth of Tony Blair's son Leo, in Observer, *May 2000* •368

Perhaps it is idealistic to suppose that any Minister might know their subject, but a passing interest is not beyond expectations.

Clare Balding, BBC sports presenter, on the lamentable performance of Richard Caborn, the new Minister for Sport, in her live sports quiz. •369

You're so back-bench, you've actually fucking fallen off. You're out by the fucking bins where I put you.

Peter Capaldi as Malcolm Tucker in The Thick Of It, *dressing down a hapless back-bench MP* •371

He was swaggering in a predatory way towards the susceptible of his conference like a gigolo eyeing the passenger deck.

Edward Pearce on Michael Portillo, in The Guardian •370

Hell, I never
vote for anybody.
I always vote against.

W.C. Fields; in Robert Lewis Taylor,
W.C. Fields *(1950)* •372

Here richly, with
   ridiculous display,
The Politician's corpse
   was laid away.
While all of his acquaintance
   sneered and slanged,
I wept: for I had longed
   to see him hanged.

British writer and Liberal politician
Hilaire Belloc (1870-1953) •373

I'll bet your father spent
the first year of your life
throwing rocks at the stork.

Groucho Marx as J Cheever Loophole in At The Circus *(1932)* •374

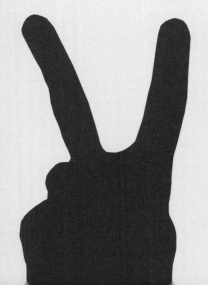

I married your mother because I wanted children. Imagine my disappointment when you arrived.

Groucho to Zeppo in
Horse Feathers •375

I don't know what Scrope Davies meant by telling you I liked children, I abominate the sight of them so much that I have always had the greatest respect for the character of Herod.
Lord Byron, letter, *30 August 1811* •376

The realisation that it was not people I disliked but children was for me one of those celebrated moments of revelation.

Philip Larkin on his adolescent epiphany;
in **Required Writing** *(1983)* •377

Oh, for an hour of Herod!

Anthony Hope at the first night of
J.M. Barrie's play, **Peter Pan;** *in*
Dennis Mackail, **The Story of JMB**
(1941) •378

You can learn many things from children. How much patience you have, for instance.

Franklin P Jones, US journalist •379

Isadora Duncan: You have the greatest brain in the world, and I have the most beautiful body; so we ought to produce the most perfect child.

George Bernard Shaw: What if the child inherits my body and your brain?

Apocryphal exchange involving George Bernard Shaw •381

It's a pity it was not the parents, rather than her, who thought of birth control.

Muriel Spark, on Marie Stopes •380

I am brought to bed of a son, who shall suck hatred to you with his milk, and that I intend to have a great many more, for the sole purpose of raising you up enemies. *Marie de Sévigné* •382

If a man's character is to be abused, say what you will, there's nobody like a relation to do the business. *William Makepeace Thackeray,* **Vanity Fair** *(1847-8)* •383

Could you possibly whistle your father and put him back on his lead, please. *Alan Ayckbourn,* **Sisterly Feelings** *(1981)* •384

Isn't it a shame when cousins marry?

A familiar retort for silencing hecklers •385

It is no use telling me there are bad aunts and good aunts. At the core, they are all alike. Sooner or later, out pops the cloven hoof. **P.G. Wodehouse, The Code of the Woosters** *(1938)* •386

Grannies are only cute on TV. In real life they're like Oxfam shops on legs. *Pamela Stephenson* •387

'It wouldn't hurt us to be nice, would it?' 'That depends on your threshold of pain.'

George S. Kaufman isn't thrilled by the prospect of a visit from his aunt; in Howard Teichmann, George S. Kaufman *(1973)* •388

But there, everything has its drawbacks, as the man said when his mother-in-law died, and they came down upon him for the funeral expenses. *Jerome K. Jerome,* Three Men in a Boat *(1889)* •389

Someone once said,
Rumbold, that education
is what is left when you
have forgotten all that
you have ever learned.
You appear to be trying to
circumvent the process by
learning as little as possible.
Alan Bennett, **Forty Years On** *(1969)* •390

I went to a girls' school
and it made me so stupid
that I could barely
remember how to breathe.
India Knight •392

Stand firm in your refusal
to remain conscious during
algebra. In real life, I assure
you, there is no such thing
as algebra. *Fran Lebowitz* •393

In the first place God made idiots. That was for practice. Then he made school boards.

Mark Twain •391

Every man should have a college
education in order to show him
how little the thing is really worth.
American writer and editor
Elbert Hubbard •394

If a man is a fool, you don't train him out of being a fool by sending him to university. You merely turn him into a trained fool, ten times more dangerous.
Novelist Desmond Bagley •395

Universities incline wits to sophistry and affectation.

Courtier and philosopher Francis Bacon, **Valerius Terminus of the Interpretation of Nature,** *(1603)* •396

Very nice sort of place, Oxford, I should think, for people that like that sort of place. They teach you to be a gentleman there. In the Polytechnic they teach you to be an engineer or such like.
George Bernard Shaw, **Man and Superman** *(1903)* •397

The average PhD thesis is nothing but the transference of bones from one graveyard to another.
American historian and folklorist **J Frank Dobie,** **A Texan in England** •398

Like so many ageing college people, Pnin had long ceased to notice the existence of students on the campus.
Vladimir Nabokov, **Paris,** *(1957)* •399

What time he can spare from the adornment of his person he devotes to the neglect of his duties.
William Thompson on Jebb, his Greek tutor at Cambridge in the 19th century •400

A graduation ceremony is an event where the commencement speaker tells thousands of students dressed in identical caps and gowns that individuality is the key to success.
American writer Cynthia Ozick, 'Women and Creativity.' (1969) •402

No academic person is ever voted into the chair until he has reached the age when he has forgotten the meaning of the word 'irrelevant'.

Francis M. Cornford, Microsmographia Academica (1908) •401

Come forth, Lazarus! And he came fifth and lost the job.

James Joyce, Ulysses (1922) •403

Prisoner before Mr Justice Darling, objecting to being referred to as 'a professional crook':
  I've only done two jobs, and each time I've been nabbed.
Lord Darling:
  It has never been suggested that you are successful in your profession.

Lord Darling; in Edward Maltby, Secrets of a Solicitor (1929) •404

Silly old fool. I pushed him into a rose bush for that.

Anna Ford recalls when Sir Robin Day told her she got a job as newsreader only because men wanted to sleep with her •405

A lawyer is a person who writes a ten-thousand-word document document and calls it a brief. *Franz Kafka* •406

I confidently expect that we [civil servants] shall continue to be grouped with mothers-in-law and Wigan Pier as one of the recognized objects of ridicule.

Edward Bridges, **Portrait of a Profession** *(1950)* •407

…all in all I'd rather have been a judge than a miner. And what is more, being a miner, as soon as you are too old and tired and sick and stupid to do the job properly, you have to go. Well, the very opposite applies with the judges.

Peter Cook, 'Sitting on a Bench', *nightclub act, 1960s* •408

Philanthropist, n. A rich (and usually bald) old gentleman who has trained himself to grin while his conscience is picking his pocket.
Ambrose Bierce, The Devil's Dictionary *(1911)* •409

If at first you don't succeed, failure may be your style.

Quentin Crisp; *in* **Sunday Telegraph** *September 1999* •410

I was just at the newly opened Creationist Museum in Kentucky... And they have this exhibit of a giant dinosaur... with a saddle on its back. Because the world is only 5,000 years old, so man and the dinosaurs had to coexist, and, of course, we rode them. A theory I thought laughable at the age of eight when I saw it on THE FLINTSTONES!
Liberal US commetator and comedian Bill Maher •411

Let the Dean and Canons lay their heads together and the thing will be done.

Sydney Smith on a proposal to surround St. Paul's cathedral with a wooden pavement; in H. Pearson, **The Smith of Smiths** *(1934)* •412

Why should we take advice on sex from the Pope? If he knows anything about it, he shouldn't.
George Bernard Shaw (attrib.) •413

Religion?
The fashionable substitute for Belief.
Oscar Wilde, **The Picture of Dorian Gray**
(1891) •414

If it turns out that there is a God,
I don't think that he's evil. But the
worst that you can say about him is
that basically he's an underachiever.
Woody Allen, **Love and Death** *(1975 film)* •417

Born again? No, I'm not. Excuse me for getting it right the first time. *Dennis Miller* •415

God, to whom, if he existed, I felt I should have nothing very polite to say.
John Mortimer, **Clinging to the Wreckage**
(1982) •418

We were skeptical Catholics. We believed Jesus walked on water. We just figured it was probably winter.

John Wing •416

Isn't God a shit?

Randolph Churchill finds God more awful
than awe-inspiring while reading the **Bible**
straight through for a bet; in Evelyn Waugh,
diary, *11 November 1944* •419

Giles: I'm not supposed to have a private life?
Buffy: No, because you're very, very old, and it's gross.

Sarah Michelle Gellar (Buffy) and Anthony Stewart Head (Giles) in Buffy the Vampire Slayer •420

The denunciation of the young is a necessary part of the hygiene of older people, and greatly assists the circulation of their blood.

Logan Pearsall Smith, Afterthoughts *(1931)* 'Age and Death' •421

Age is deformed, youth unkind,
We scorn their bodies, they our mind.
Thomas Bastard, Chrestoleros *(1598)* •422

Here lies
Ezekial Aikle
Aged 102
The Good
Die Young

Epitaph found in East Dalhousie, Nova Scotia •423

Only think of Mrs Holder's being dead! Poor woman, she has done the only thing in the world she could possibly do to make one cease to abuse her.

Jane Austen, letter to her sister, Cassandra •424

He'd make a lovely corpse.

Charles Dickens, Martin Chuzzlewit *(1844)* •425

Waldo is one of those people who would be enormously improved by death.

Saki, **Beasts and Superbeasts** *(1914)* •426

I hope I don't die before Harry Secombe. I don't want him singing at my funeral.

Spike Milligan jokes at memorial service for Alf Garnett creator Johnny Speight; also attrib. as a fax sent by Milligan to Secombe •427

What I like about Clive
Is that he is no longer alive.
There is a great deal to be said
For being dead.

Edmund Clerihew Bentley, 'Clive' (1905) •428

God was very good to the world.
He took her from us.

Bette Davis on Miriam Hopkins •429

Well it only proves what they always say — give the public something they want to see, and they'll come out for it.

Red Skelton comments on the crowds attending the funeral of movie tycoon Harry Cohn, March 1958; attrib. •430

Darling, if you want to talk bollocks and discover the meaning of life, you're better off downing a bottle of whiskey. At least that way, you're unconscious by the time you start to take yourself seriously.

Patsy (Joanna Lumley) dispenses advice in 'The End', Absolutely Fabulous, *1995* •431

I hate all sports as
rabidly as a person
who likes sports
hates common sense.

H.L. Mencken •432

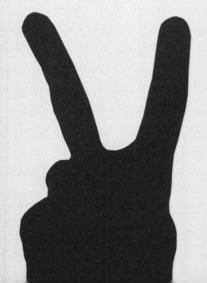

He wears a No. 10 jersey.
I thought it was his position
but it turns out to be his IQ.

George Best on Paul Gascoigne •433

He's been very, very
lucky; an average
player who came
into the game
when it was short
of personalities.

George Best on Kevin Keegan •434

He can't kick with his left
foot. He doesn't score many
goals. He can't head a ball.
And he can't tackle. Apart
from that he's all right.

George Best's appraisal of
David Beckham •435

Becks hasn't changed since I've known him. He's always been a flash Cockney git.

Ryan Giggs' wry comment on Becks' love of the limelight •436

I've just seen Gary Lineker shake hands with Jurgen Klinsmann — it's a wonder Klinsmann hasn't fallen over. *Ron Atkinson* •437

He's the worst finisher since Devon Loch. When he's in a clear shooting position he's under orders to do just one thing… pass.

Atkinson on his own player, Carlton Palmer •438

Carlton Palmer can trap the ball further than I can kick it.

And again •439

The ideal soccer board of directors should be made up of three men; two dead, and the other dying. *Tommy Docherty* •440

Tony Hateley had it all. The only thing he lacked was ability. *Docherty on Tony Hateley* •441

He didn't look anything like a professional athlete when I first clapped eyes on him. In fact, there were times when he barely resembled a member of the human race. *Brian Clough on former Forest winger John Robertson* •442

It's just like playing alongside Barbara Streisand. *Mike Summerbee suggests Rodney Marsh isn't the best team player, 1973* •443

Someone once said you could write down Barry's knowledge of management on a postage stamp. I would say you need to fold the stamp in half.

Steve Claridge on Barry Fry •444

A complete and utter shit.

Barry Fry on former Barnet chairman, Stan Flashman •445

You are talking about a man who spelt his name wrong on his transfer request.

Gary Megson on Jason Roberts •446

Harry Redknapp lookalike requires cash for corrective surgery to avoid Bagpuss jibes.

Private Eye spoof ad •447

A bag of shite. My grandmother would do better, on acid, with a Toblerone stuck up her arse.
Liam Gallagher, 2005, on the travails of the England football team •448

They could put a parking meter next to Alan Hansen and I'd find it more interesting watching it click round.

Rodney Marsh is spot-on for once in his assessment of Peter Schmeichel's ability as a TV pundit •449

If you've all got a passport clap your hands.

Terrace chant aimed at Fulham chairman, Mohamed Al-Fayed •450

Golf is not a sport.
Golf is men in ugly
pants, walking.
Robin Williams •451

I played like
Doug Saunders
and putted like
Colonel Sanders.
Chi Chi Rodríguez •452

It would be an act of
unimaginable masochism
to plough through a tape
of Alliss commentary.
*Marina Hyde on golf commentator Peter
Alliss, in* The Guardian •453

My God, it looks
like a wax museum!
George Low turns up at his first seniors event •454

When Langer practices on his
own, he can hold up a fourball.
Dave Musgrove, Bernhard's caddie •455

*American tourist (having just
sliced his tee shot out of bounds):*
In our country, we call that
a Mulligan. What you call
it over here?
St Andrew's caddie:
A three. •456

137

Colin Montgomerie
has a face like
a warthog that
has been stung
by a wasp. *David Feherty* •457

I don't know him but
I've seen him smile and
that's quite enough to put
me off wanting to know
anything about him.
Feherty on Phil Mickelson •458

I keep thinking that
I might go out and
play like Jack Nicklaus,
but instead it's more
like Jacques Tati.
Feherty on himself •459

Like an octopus
falling out of a tree.

Feherty assesses Jim Furyk's swing •460

Top hats look 100% ridiculous on anybody, but on, for example, Willie Carson, it's like attaching a factory chimney to a bungalow.

Giles Smith, TV critic, on the Royal enclosure at Ascot •461

Rowntree's ears are a stark warning of the aesthetic dangers of prolonged exposure to the rugby scrum… they resemble those indeterminate, gristly things given to puppies to chew on.

Derek Potter, 2002, from **Down Among The Head Men** •462

His shyness is derivative of not having a high intellect.

Scott Gibbs on Welsh rugby union colleague Gavin Henson •463

The human equivalent of beige.

Linda Smith on Tim Henman •464

Journalist:
 Have you and Stacey split up?
McEnroe:
 I'd like you to quote that you guys are shit.

McEnroe shoots from the hip •465

The little dictator with the Beatles haircut.

Paul Weaver (The Guardian) *on Bernie Ecclestone* •466

A drunkard, a glutton and a hellraiser.

Ed Smith on Babe Ruth, **Playing Hard Ball,** *(2002)* •467

Gower: Do you want Gatt a foot wider?
Cowdrey (the bowler): No, he'd burst.

Chris Cowdrey's response to his captain's suggestion that Mike Gatting be moved in the slip cordon •468

Bad luck, Sir — you were just getting settled in.

Yorkshire's Fred Trueman to a University batsman, clean bowled first ball after lengthy 'limbering-up' and gardening at the wicket •469

Captain: I want a fielder right under Hussain's nose.
Ian Healy: That could mean anywhere within three miles.

Nasser Hussain told this one himself •470

Mark Waugh: Fuck me, look who it is. Mate, what are you doing out here? There's no way you're good enough to play for England.
Jimmy Ormond: Maybe not, but at least I'm the best player in my family.
Ashes, 2001 •471

Shane Warne: I've been waiting for two years to have another bowl at you.
Daryl Cullinan: Looks like you spent most of it eating.
Reported by Simon Hughes in Yakking Round The World •472

So how's your wife, and my kids?
Rodney Marsh to Ian Botham •473

Greg Thomas (After beating the bat):
   It's red, round and weighs about five ounces.

Viv Richards (after hammering the next ball out of the ground):
   You know what it looks like, now go and fetch it.
   Viv shows why he's never an ideal target for sledging •474

Glenn McGrath: Why are you so fucking fat?
Eddo Brandes: Because every time I fuck your wife she gives me a biscuit.
   Zimbabwean tail-ender Brandes fails to be intimidated by McGrath's abuse •475

WE LOATHED:
Billy Bowden's Histrionics: the attention-seeking umpire was outmanoeuvred by Rudi Koertzen.

WE LOATHED:
Cricket Bling: Messrs Pietersen and Warne take note: diamonds are a girl's best friend.

WE LOATHED:
There Goes Another Pigeon: Henry Blofeld's fruity eccentricities on Test Match Special.

From **Observer Sport Monthly's** *round-up of the 2005 Ashes series* •476

I am not the greatest conductor in
this country. On the other hand,
I am better than any damned foreigner.

Sir Thomas Beecham (1879-1961) •477

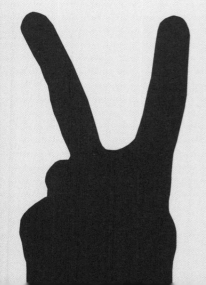

Why do we have to have all these third-rate foreign conductors around — when we have so many second-rate ones of our own?

Thomas Beecham; L. Ayre,
Wit of Music *(1966)* •478

Beethoven's last quartets were written by a deaf man and should only be listened to by a deaf man.

Sir Thomas Beecham on
Ludwig van Beethoven •479

I nearly trod in some once.

Sir Thomas Beecham, on Stockhausen •480

I didn't know he'd been knighted. I knew he'd been doctored.

Thomas Beecham on fellow composer
Malcolm Sargent's knighthood; attrib. •481

What can you do with it? It's like a lot of yaks jumping about.

Thomas Beecham on the third movement of
Beethoven's Seventh Symphony; in Harold
Atkins and Archie Newman, **Beecham**
Stories *(1978)* •482

By God, no, if it had been I should have run away myself.

The Duke of Wellington, on being asked whether a performance of Beethoven's The Battle of Vitoria *resembled the real battle* •483

Wagner has lovely moments but awful quarters of an hour.

Giacchino Rossini, said to Emile Naumann, April 1867, in E. Naumann, Italienische Tondichter *(1883)* •484

I have been told that Wagner's music is better than it sounds.

Mark Twain, (atttrib.) •485

The music of Wagner imposes mental tortures that only algebra has a right to inflict.

Paul de Saint-Victor on Richard Wagner in La Presse •486

Liszt's orchestral music is an insult to art. It is gaudy musical harlotry, savage and incoherent bellowings.

Boston Gazette *on Franz Liszt* •487

I can compare Le Carnaval Romain by Berlioz to nothing but the caperings and gibberings of a big baboon, over-excited by a dose of alcoholic stimulus.
George Templeton Strong; diary entry •488

Very vile — a catarrhal or sternutatory concerto. One frequently recurring phrase is a graphic instrumentation of a fortissimo sneeze, and a long passage is evidently meant to suggest a protracted, agonised bravura on the pocket handkerchief.
George Templeton Strong on a concerto by Franz Liszt; diary entry •489

The musical equivalent of blancmange.

Bernard Levin on Frederick Delius •490

He is like a man who sits on a stove and then complains that his backside is burning.
Gilbert on Sullivan •491

Another week's rehearsal with WSG & I should have gone raving mad. I had already ordered some straw for my hair.
Sullivan on Gilbert •492

His requiem is patiently borne only by the corpse.
George Bernard Shaw on Brahms •493

I liked your opera.
I think I'll set it to music.

Ludwing van Beethoven
to a fellow composer •494

People are wrong when they say the opera isn't what it used to be. It is what it used to be — that's what's wrong with it.

Noël Coward, **Design for Living** *(1933)*
•495

(He) might well have loaded up a shotgun with several thousand notes of various length and discharged them against the side of a blank wall.

Edward Moore on prokofiev's
The Love of Three Oranges •496

I allowed twenty-four hours to elapse before writing this review: if I had been forced to produce it immediately after leaving the opera house, my language would have been distressingly intemperate. To put it mildly, then, this was the worst production that I can remember having experienced of any opera, and the only completely unmoving one of Fidelio…

Throughout the evening, the stage looked an absolute mess, comically so when the grim reaper and the devil arrived in stilts in the final scene. The audience, which until then had behaved itself surprisingly well, finally hooted with glee when the devil's curtains managed to close around Pizarro only with a little help from Pizarro itself.

I do advise the hard-hearted to go and see this Fidelio: they'll have a good laugh.

Charles Osborne on Beethoven's opera
Fidelio *at the Royal Opera House, London.*
In **Jewish Chronicle,** *July 1986* •497

"A crude monstrosity, a serpent which continues to move about, refusing to expire, and even when bleeding to death still threshes around angrily and vainly with its tail.

Charles Osborne on a production of
A German music magazine reviews
Beethoven's 2nd Symphony •498

The third movement began with a dog howling at midnight, proceeded to imitate the repurgations of the less-refined lower-middle-class type of water-closet cistern, modulating thence into the mass snoring of a naval dormitory around dawn — and concluded inconsequentially with the cello reproducing the screech of an ungreased wheelbarrow.

Alan Dent on Bela Bartók •499

This version takes place not in ancient Peking, but in the interior of a corrugated iron drum. Its characters are dressed in a variety of styles, ranging over 1,000 years of fashion Some of them creep around in slow motion, while the young Prince of Persia, who is about to be executed, engages in simulated homo-erotic sex with his executioner. The courtiers Ping, Pang and Pong are portrayed as figures out of American vaudeville… and a huge banner in Act II informs us, unnecessarily and inaccurately, that 3 Enigmas = Death. It gets worse.

***Charles Osborne on a production of Puccini's opera* Turandot, *at the London Coliseum,** December 1995* •500

Swans sing before they die: 'twere no bad thing Should certain persons die before they sing.

Samuel Taylor Coleridge, 'On a Volunteer Singer' *(1834)* •501

Last year I gave several lectures on 'Intelligence and the Appreciation of Music Among Animals.' Today I am going to speak to you about 'Intelligence and Appreciation of Music Among Critics.' The subject is very similar.

Erik Satie (1866-1925); in Nat Shapiro (ed.) **An Encylopedia of Quotations about Music** *(1978)* •502

I have just read your lousy review buried in the back pages. You sound like a frustrated old man who never made a success, an eight-ulcer man on a four-ulcer job, and all four ulcers working. I have never met you, but if I do you'll need a new nose and plenty of beefsteak and perhaps a support below.

Harry S. Truman to **Washington Post** *music critic Paul Hume* •503

Jazz: Music invented for the torture of imbeciles.

Harry van Dyke •504

I don't like country music — but don't mean to denigrate those who do. For those people who like country music, denigrate means to put down.

Bob Newhart •505

She ought to be arrested for loitering in front of an orchestra.

Bette Midler on Helen Reddy •506

Presley sounded like Jayne Mansfield looked — blowsy and loud and low.

Julie Burchill •507

They are, in my mind, responsible for most of the degeneration that has happened, not only musically but also in the sense of youth orientation and politically, too. They are the people who made it first publicly acceptable to spit in the eye of authority.

Reverend Pat Robertson? No, Frank Sinatra on The Beatles •508

Oh, I get it. You don't want to be cute any more.

Bob Dylan's reaction to **Sgt Pepper's** •509

To hear Tom Jones sing Sinatra's *My Way* is roughly akin to watching Tab Hunter play King Lear. Mr Jones is, in the words of his own hit, not unusual… at least not as a singer, as a sex symbol he is nothing short of inexplicable.

Sheridan Morley, in Punch •510

If I found her floating in my pool, I'd punish my dog.

Joan Rivers on Yoko Ono •511

This man has child-bearing lips. *Joan Rivers on Mick Jagger* •512

He moves like a parody between a majorette girl and Fred Astaire.

Truman Capote on Mick Jagger •513

At the Grammy Awards, Keith Richards became the first performer ever to accept a posthumous award in Britain.

Jay Leno on 'strolling bone' Keith Richards, **The Tonight Show,** *NBC* •514

Actually, I never liked Dylan's kind of music before, I always thought he sounded like Yogi Bear.

Mick Ronson •515

I think that's just another word for a washed-up has-been.

Bob Dylan, on being an 'Icon' •516

Dylan to me is the perfect symbol of the anti-artist in our society. He is against everything — the last resort of someone who doesn't really want to change the world… Dylan's songs accept the world as it is.

Ewan MacColl on Bob Dylan,
Melody Maker, *1965* •517

Bob Dylan impresses me about as much as… well, I was gonna say a slug but I like slugs.

Don Van Vliet, aka Captain Beefheart •518

He plays four-and-a-half hour sets, That's torture. Does he hate his audience?

John Lydon about Bruce Springsteen •519

He was so mean it hurt him to go to the bathroom.

Britt Ekland about Rod Stewart •520

They didn't look like humans. They looked like foetuses. I felt physically ill when I saw them on TV.

The ever-restrained Julie Burchill on Bay City Rollers •521

He has Van Gogh's ear for music.

Orson Welles on '70s pop star Donny Osmond •522

Five bowls of muesli looking for a spoon.

The New Musical Express on Yes •523

Like a foul alignment of all the black planets, this collection of 95-97 material culled from the *Keys to Ascension I* and *II* albums, saw all the important members of Yes [...] reunited to wreak havoc on the world. Chords are played at random, tunes change tempo for no other reason than that is what happens in symphonies and tracks are long just for longness's sake... The fact that they had a hit single as recently as 15 years ago should serve as a warning to us all that this sort of thing could strike at any moment.

David Quantick reviews Yes's album Keys to the Studio *in* **Q Magazine,** *September 2001* •524

In a cybernetic fit of rage
She pissed off to another age
She lives in 1999
With her new boyfriend,
  a blob of slime.
Each time I see a translucent face
I remember the monster
  from outer space.

John Cooper Clarke, I Married A Monster from Outer Space, *1978* •525

If you looked up the word pretentious in the dictionary, you could possibly see a picture of Emerson, Lake and Palmer.
Carl Palmer •526

I'm not offended at all because I know I'm not a dumb blonde. I also know I'm not blonde.
Dolly Parton brushes her critics aside; in M. Palmer, **Small Talk, Big Names: 40 Years of Rock Quotes** *(1993)* •527

All legs and hair with a mouth that could swallow the whole stadium and the hot-dog stand.
Laura Lee Davies on Tina Turner •528

You have to admire her. She hides her lack of talent so well.
Manola Blahnik, shoemaker, on Madonna •529

She's so hairy, when she lifted her arm I thought it was Tina Turner in her armpit.

Joan Rivers on Madonna •530

Bambi with testosterone.

Owen Gleiberman on Prince, in Entertainment Weekly •531

He looks like a dwarf who's been dipped in a bucket of pubic hair.

Boy George on Prince •532

Lovesexy, it has to be said, is a turgid collection of inconclusive riffs and weak melodies, decorated to distraction by harsh and flashy ornamentation.

David Toop, on Prince's album Love Sexy, *in the* Sunday Times, *22 May 1988* •533

Michael Jackson's album was only called 'Bad' because there wasn't enough room on the sleeve for Pathetic.

Prince •535

If you, like, make out with a frog, then you turn into Prince.

Butthead •534

After meeting Bono, it made me want to
give up being in a rock & roll band.
Dave Grohl of Nirvana (1992) •536

The Celine Dion we know and love is a
handsome woman. That's not the
way I remember her from Eurovision.

*Surely Mr Wogan isn't suggesting
a bit of nip and tuck?* •537

It's hardly Paul McCartney leaving The Beatles.
Noel Gallagher, on Bonehead's departure from Oasis (1999) •538

I just wish Eddie Vedder
would get on with it
and kill himself.

*Noel Gallagher of Oasis on the
Pearl Jam frontman, 1996* •539

She's got a face like a satellite dish and ankles like my granny's.

Robbie Williams on British pop star Sophie Ellis Bextor •540

And yes, making Posh Spice look dumb didn't turn out to be all that hard.

The Guardian *columnist Zoe Williams* •541

We made it easy for them to come and nick things from us. They're sticky tape on a duck's arse.

The Sex Pistols' John Lydon questions Green Day's originality •542

The still-born brainchild of Korn bassist Reginald Fieldy Arvizu, Rock 'n' Roll Gangster is an utterly unlikeable gangsta-rap pastiche. When not tiresomely trumpeting his titanic weed intake, Fieldy stumbles through sterilised sex rhymes and banal B-boy bragging so devoid of charm or wit that they make the similarly salacious Kid Rock sound like Stephen Fry in comparison.

Dan Silver on the album Rock 'n' Roll Gangster *by Fieldy's Dreams, in* Q *magazine, January 2002* •543

In the 18-year old wake of David Bowie's 'Pin-Ups', few artists have been foolish enough to do a covers album. Duran Duran were the last notable culprits with 1995's inexplicable 'Thank You'; and now Simple Minds have decided to come after them… Really, to call this a turkey would be unfair to the birds who share the name.

John Harris on Simple Minds' **Neon Lights**; *in* Q *magazine, October 2001* •544

Three tracks in this truly lamentable opus and you'll have lost the will to live; four tracks and you'll be weeping openly into your coffee cup.

James Cooper on heavy metal band Solstice's album Lamentations; *in* Kerrang, *August 2001* •545

Macho rap-rock from the UK. Horrible, horrible. This is the sound of five men in competition to prove who has the most testosterone.

Emma Johnston on nu-metal band Lillydamnwhite (album Eviscerate) *in* Kerrang, *July 2001* •546

This tragic bombardment of tuneless metal cliché fails to move in any direction other than towards the bin.

Steve Beebee on Debase's album Domination, *in* Kerrang, *October 2001* •547

"

From Dylan to Sid Vicious to Eminem, the real X Factor has nothing to do with what old people think of you. It's about attitude — and those who have it don't burst into tears and beg for one more chance to ingratiate themselves.

AA Gill finds the X factor sadly lacking in The X Factor •548

If you'd sung like this 2,000 years ago, people would've stoned you.

Simon Cowell on particularly splenetic form on The X Factor •549

Oh, the self-importance of fading stars. Never mind, they will all be black holes one day.

Jeffrey Bernard; in **The Spectator,** *July 1992* •550

> Lillie wasn't exactly a beauty, though her eyes were; she just happened to be born in a day when standards were far lower and less exacting.

Rachel Ferguson on Lillie Langtry •551

George: A Charlie Chaplin film! Oh, I love old Chappers, don't you, Cap?
Blackadder: Unfortunately, no I don't. I find his films about as funny as getting an arrow through the neck and then discovering there's a gas bill tied to it.
Hugh Laurie and Rowan Atkinson in **Blackadder Goes Forth,** *(1989)* •552

Can't act. Slightly bald. Also dances.
A studio official comments on Fred Astaire; quoted by Bob Thomas Astaire *(1985)* •553

Katharine Hepburn: Thank goodness I don't have to act with you any more.
John Barrymore: I didn't know you ever had, darling.
The loving couple, after filming A Bill of Divorcement *(1932)* •554

She sounds more and more like Donald Duck.
Bette Davis on Katharine Hepburn •555

I refuse to play golf with Errol Flynn.
If I want to play with a prick, I'll
play with my own. *W.C. Fields* •556

That man's ears make him look like
a taxi-cab with both doors open.
*Howard Hughes Jr., of Clark Gable; in
Charles Higham and Joel Greenberg,*
Celluloid Muse *(1969)* •557

Dietrich? That contraption! She was one
of the beautiful-but-dumb girls, like me,
but she belonged to the category of those
who thought they were smart and fooled
other people into believing it.
Louise Brooks on Marlene Dietrich •558

Doris Day is as wholesome as a bowl
of cornflakes and at least as sexy.

Dwight Macdonald, US critic •559

When the bespangled Cyd Charisse wraps her phenomenal legs around Fred Astaire, she can be forgiven everything — even the fact that she reads her lines as if she learned them phonetically.
A sting in the tail from Pauline Kael in a review of **The Band Wagon** *(1953)* •560

It's sometimes discouraging to see all of a director's movies, because there's so much repetition. The auteurists took this to be a sign of a director's artistry, that you could recognize his movies. But it can also be a sign that he's a hack. *Pauline Kael* •561

Cecil B. de Mille
Rather against his will,
Was persuaded to leave Moses
Out of The War of the Roses.
Nicholas Bentley on Hollywood impresario C.B. de Mille •562

Charlton Heston has a bad memory.
He still thinks he's Moses parting the Red Sea.
Barbara Stanwyck •563

A man who can part the Red Sea but apparently not his own hairpiece.
Dick Vosburgh and Denis King on Charlton Heston; **Beauty and the Beards** *(2001)* •564

Marilyn Monroe was good at playing abstract confusion in the same way that a midget is good at being short.

Clive James •565

She has breasts of granite and a mind like a Gruyere cheese.

Billy Wilder on Marilyn Monroe •566

A vacuum with nipples.

Otto Preminger on Marilyn Monroe •567

It's like kissing Hitler.

Tony Curtis gives his verdict on kissing Marilyn Monroe;
A. Hunter, **Tony Curtis** *(1985)* •568

[Tony Curtis] only said that about kissing Hitler because I wore prettier dresses than he did.

Marilyn Monroe •569

I miss her. It was like going to the dentist, making a picture with her.

Billy Wilder on Monroe •570

Most of the time he sounds like he
has a mouthful of wet toilet paper.

Rex Reed on Marlon Brando •571

I have a face that would stop a sundial.

Charles Laughton •572

I have a face like an elephants behind.

Charles Laughton •573

If, sir, I possessed , as you suggest the power of
conveying unlimited sexual attraction
through the potency of my voice, I would
not be reduced to accepting a miserable
pittance from the BBC for interviewing
a faded female in a damp basement.

*Gilbert Harding's reply to Mae West's manager, who had asked 'Can't you
sound a bit more sexy when you interview her?'. In S.Grenfell,*
Gilbert Harding by his Friends *(1961)* •574

The best time I ever had with Joan Crawford
was when I pushed her down the stairs in
What Ever Happened to Baby Jane?
Bette Davis •575

She was good at what she did, at what she settled for.
Bette Davis on Joan Crawford •576

Joan always cries a lot. Her tear ducts
must be very close to her bladder.
Bette Davis on Joan Crawford •577

She slept with every male star at MGM, except Lassie.
Bette Davis on Joan Crawford •578

Poor Bette, it appears she's never had a happy day, or night, in her life.
Joan Crawford on Bette Davis •579

Take away the pop eyes, the cigarette and those
funny clipped words and what have you got?
Joan Crawford on her old chum, Bette Davis •580

> You look at Ernest Borgnine
> and you think to yourself:
> was there anybody else
> hurt in the accident?
>
> *Don Rickles* •581

Mia Farrow? I always knew Frank would end up in bed with a boy.
Ava Gardner is disparaging about ex-husband Frank Sinatra's latest squeeze •582

> The rudest man I ever met,
> andunattractive — pock-marked
> as an Easter Island statue.
>
> *Broadcaster Libby Purves on Richard Burton* •583

Her face could launch
a thousand dredgers.

Jack De Manio on Glenda Jackson •584

> You're so vain, you probably
> think this song is about you.
>
> *Carly Simon's song, reputedly about Warren Beatty* •585

Michael Caine can out-act any,
well nearly any, telephone kiosk
you care to mention.

Hugh Leonard, Irish playwright •586

Michael Caine compares himself
to Gene Hackman. This is foolish.
Hackman is an intimidating and
dangerous actor. Mr. Caine is
about as dangerous as Laurel
and Hardy, or indeed both, and
as intimidating as Shirley Temple.

Richard Harris •587

He has the attention span of a bolt of lightning.
Robert Redford on Butch Cassidy… *co-star Paul Newman* •588

Robert Redford has turned almost alarmingly blond — he's gone past platinum, he must be into plutonium; his hair is co-ordinated with his teeth. *Pauline Kael, 1976* •589

Poor little man. They made him out of lemon Jell-O and there he is.

Adela Rogers St John on Robert Redford •590

To know her is not necessarily to love her.
Rex Reed on notorious 'diva' Barbra Streisand •591

He is to acting what Liberace was to pumping iron.
Rex Reed on Sylvester Stallone •592

You thought Dirk Benedict had problems in TV's Battlestar Galactica? In Scavenger Hunt, he really had problems — in one mercifully brief scene, he was out-acted by a jock-strap.
Rona Barrett on Dirk Benedict •593

What do you mean, heart attack? You've got to have a heart before you can have an attack.

Billy Wilder on Peter Sellers' coronary •594

Trying for the mystery of glamour, Julie Andrews merely coarsens her shining nice-girl image, becoming a nasty Girl Guide. *Pauline Kael* •595

Like Dionysus crossed with a convent girl on her first bender.

Pauline Kael assesses Prince's performance in **Purple Rain;** *in* **The New Yorker,** *August 1984* •596

I once described him as a brown condom full of walnuts.
Clive James on Arnold Schwarzenegger; in **Daily Mail** *August 2003* •597

A fellow with the inventiveness of Albert Einstein but with the attention span of Daffy Duck.

Tom Shales on Robin Williams •598

Demi Moore is the Arnold Schwarzenegger of women.

Candace Bushnell •599

Ken Russell casts himself in the title role of his own film, *The Secret Life of Arnold Bax*, and gives a portrayal so dire that I suspect he may have had to perform sexual favours for himself on the casting couch in order to get the part.

Victor Lewis-Smith •600

It's a new low for actresses when you have to wonder what's between her ears instead of her legs.

Katherine Hepburn, after Sharon Stone's infamous leg-uncrossing, sans knickers, in Basic Instinct •601

Jean-Claude van Damme exudes the charisma of a packet of Cup-a-Soup. *Jonathan Romney* •602

It is like kissing the Berlin Wall.
Helena Bonham Carter on acting with Woody Allen •603

All my life I wanted to look like Liz Taylor. Now
I find that Liz Taylor is beginning to look like me.
Drag queen Divine •604

Elizabeth Taylor's so fat, she puts mayonnaise on aspirin.
Joan Rivers •605

I don't like actors, I just don't like them.
I met Warren Beatty one time and I thought:
"This is one of the creepiest puke-asses
I've ever met in my life."
Mickey Rourke — not your usual luvvie — in 1994 •606

Jack Warner has oilcloth
pockets so he can steal soup.
Wilson Mizner •607

I think that's what they
call professional courtesy.
*Herman J. Mankiewicz, on hearing that a
Hollywood agent had swum safely in
shark-infested waters; attrib.* •608

> ## The only Greek Tragedy I know.
> *Billy Wilder on Spyros Skouras, Head of Fox Studios; attrib., perhaps apocryphal* •609

Slimelight
Long-serving **New Yorker** *film critic*
Pauline Kael, on Chaplin's **Limelight** *(1952)* •610

I would like to recommend this film to those who can stay interested in Ronald Colman's amnesia for two hours and who could with pleasure eat a bowl of Yardley's shaving soap for breakfast. *James Agee, reviewing* **Random Harvest,** *(1942)* •611

So mincing as to border on baby talk.

Bosley Crowther on It's A Wonderful Life *(1946)* •612

Several tons of dynamite are set off in this picture; none of it under the right people.

James Agee finds fault with Tycoon *(1947);* *in* The Nation, *February 1948* •613

The old master has turned out another Hitchcock and bull story, in which the mystery is not so much who done it as who cares. Time *magazine on* Hitchcock's Vertigo *(1958)* •614

The only really satisfactory way to dispose of *Peeping Tom* would be to shovel it up and flush it swiftly down the nearest sewer. Even then, the stench would remain.

Derek Hill on **Peeping Tom** *(1960)* •615

Let my people go!
Mort Sahl at a viewing of **Exodus** *(1960)*; *attrib. 1961*•616

They only got two things right in *Lawrence of Arabia*: the camels and the sand. *Lowell Thomas (1962)* •617

I had never numbered Bergman among the slyer contemporary wags; all the same, I expected something slightly less elephantine than tinted Norman Wisdom. What goings-on! I gape in amazement, remarks one of the subtitles, and I can't say I blame it.

Kenneth Tynan on Ingmar Bergman film **Now About These Women** *(1964)* •618

This dingy charade spends two hours
repeating a message already familiar in the
first twenty minutes: All they want is my body.
Carroll Baker supplies the body, if not the erotic
incandescence that made them want it. She didn't
die of pneumonia, says her agent after the girl
gasps her last, she died of life. In fact, she died
of neither. Nothing reveals the essential mendacity
of Harlow more clearly than its refusal to admit
that a Hollywood sex symbol could die of
uremic poisoning. Angela Lansbury, Raf Vallone,
and Red Buttons are among those who
officiate at this shoddy exhumation.
*Kenneth Tynan on a 1965 'biopic' of
Hollywood actress Jean Harlow* •619

The nuns, as always in American films, are average
American housewives inexplicably veiled in black;
a twinkling bunch of good-hearted gossips, healthily
unconcerned with sex. They sing all their wimples off,
including — strangely enough — the Mother Superior,
who bursts into full contralto shortly after informing
us that singing in the cloister is forbidden.
Kenneth Tynan on **The Sound of Music** *(1965)* •620

Mister Moses is the one about the African village that must either quit its ancestral home to accommodate the new dam or stay and get drowned. Like most films, it stars Carroll Baker. The running time is 115 minutes; the walking-out time is much earlier. The weather throughout is excellent.

Kenneth Tynan on Mister Moses *(1965)* •621

Wasn't there perhaps one little Von Trapp who didn't want to sing his head off, or who screamed that he wouldn't act out little glockenspiel routines for Papa's party guests, or who got nervous and threw up if he had to get on stage?

Wishful thinking from Pauline Kael as she reviews The Sound of Music *(1965)* •622

Then came *Easy Rider*, a disaster in the history of film…

David Thomson, critic, on Easy Rider *(1969)* •623

The movie is of an unbelievable badness; it brings back clichés you didn't know you knew… You can't get angry at something this stupefying; it seems to have been made by trolls.

Pauline Kael on Song of Norway, *a biopic of composer Edvard Grieg, (1970)* •624

I still can't believe I saw this freak show, a self-consciously mod, disjointed patchwork of leers, vulgarity, and general ineptness.

William Wolf on Myra Breckenridge, *in* Cue, *(1970)* •625

At Hélène's party, during which her sensational norks are practically on the table among the sweetmeats, Pierre is asked to do a worried version of the bug-eyed act Sid James turns on when he is abruptly shoved up against Barbara Windsor.

Clive James on a BBC production of Tolstoy's War and Peace *(1972)* •626

The jokes are tired and can often be seen dragging their feet towards us a mile off; when they finally arrive, we are more apt to commiserate than laugh.

John Simon on Woody Allen's Annie Hall *(1977)* •627

To be fair, the movie does show a certain charm in its relentlessly stupid grasp of the obvious. When Frampton sings *The Long and Winding Road*, for example, he is walking down a long and winding road. You keep laughing and thinking it can't get any worse. But it does. *Charles M. Young on Beatles movie* Sgt. Pepper's Lonely Hearts Club Band *(1978) in* Rolling Stone *magazine* •628

Table for Five would be an ideal movie to watch on a plane; at least they provide free sick bags.

Simon Rose reviews **Table for Five** *(1983)* •629

The picture is like a slightly psychopathic version of an old Saturday-afternoon serial, with Harry sneering at the scum and cursing them before he shoots them with his king-size custom-made 44 Auto Mag. He (Clint Eastwood) takes particular pleasure in kicking and bashing a foul-mouthed lesbian; we get the idea. In his eyes, she's worse than her male associates, because women are supposed to be ladies. Eastwood's disapproval of her impropriety sits a little bit oddly in a movie with sub-barnyard jokes about a little bulldog's hindquarters and a laugh-fest centering on a man shot in the genitals and a frankfurter covered in ketchup.

Pauline Kael on **Sudden Impact** *(1983),* **in The New Yorker,** *January 1984* •630

What kind of a title for a movie is *Greystoke: The Legend of Tarzan, Lord of the Apes*? A pompous, foolish one. There can't be many people who will remember this title, or many theatres that are equipped with colons for their marquees, either. *Pauline Kael on* Greystoke… *(1983)in* **The New Yorker,** *April 1984* •631

Makes you look for something lighter and wittier such as a documentary on the Khmer Rouge.
Simon Rose on Shanghai Surprise *(1986)* •632

A wet piece of kitsch.

Pauline Kael on Rain Man *(1988)* •633

Here is the ideal date movie, assuming you're dating a psychopath sadist with a high tolerance for dilly-dallying… The younger actors all seem fresh off the campus of the James Woods-Willem Dafoe Institute For Acting Surly, Nervous and Dishevelled.
Ralph Novak on Reservoir Dogs *(1991)* •634

What did I think of *Titanic*? I'd rather have been on it.

Miles Kruger assesses 1997's Titanic •635

Proof, if proof were needed, that the return of the dumb teen comedy genre may be on its last legs, Danny Leiner's woefully inept buddy flick redefines unfunny in ways you never knew possible. Mistaking repetition of dialogue for a fruitful means of laughter grabbing, the misadventures of the two stoners searching aimlessly for their missing motor takes in charmless, witless, and painfully dull in equal measures, without ever throwing in an original idea in its 82-minute running time.

Risible, dire, or just about any synonym for Godawful you want to come up with… This unmitigated stream of celluloid ordure could draw a chalk outline round its corpse. All together: 'Dude, where's my refund?'

William Thomas on Dude, Where's My Car? *(2000) In* Empire *magazine, March 2001* •636

No intelligent person could like this film.

Andrew O'Hagan, of The Daily Telegraph, *on* Pearl Harbour *(2001)* •637

189

The problem with *Sex Lives of the Potato Men* is it is absolutely, indescribably horrible, vulgar, stupid, tawdry, depressing, embarassing, filthy, vile, stinky, repugnant, slimy, unclean, nasty, degenerative and mind-numbing.

Mark Kermode, BBC film critic.
But did you enjoy it, Mark? •638

Disappears up its own fundamental implausibility.

The Observer's *Philip French*
on Dream House *(2011)* •640

Transformers: The Revenge of The Fallen is beyond bad, it carves out its own category of godawfulness.
Peter Travers in Rolling Stone *(2009)* •639

This latest *Twilight* is a freakish hybrid: part medical horror, part cheesy Victoria's Secret catalogue shoot.

Kate Muir in The Times *on*
Twilight: Breaking Dawn *(2011)* •641

My dear, good is not the word.

Max Beerbohm, 'reassuring' a leading lady after a particularly bad first night; attrib. •642

Go on failing. Go on. Only next time, try to fail better.

Samuel Beckett finds a use for advice given in his 1983 play Westward Ho ("Ever tried. Ever failed. No matter. Try again. Fail again. Fail better") when during a rehearsal at the Royal Court an actor lamented, "I'm failing"; in Tony Richardson, **Long Distance Runner** *(1993)* •643

That popular Stage-playes… are all sinful, heathenish, lewde, ungodly Spectacles, and most pernicious Corruptions; condemned in all ages, as intolerable Mischiefes to Churches, to Republickes, to the manners, mindes, and soules of men. And that the Profession of Play-poets, of Stage-players; together with the penning, acting, and frequenting of Stage-playes, are unlawful, infamous, and misbeseeming Christians.

William Prynne (c.1600-1669) •644

Mr Ainley played the old codger like a toastmaster celebrating his golden wedding.

James Agate on Henry Ainley as Prospero, 1934 •645

An ego like a raging tooth.

W.B. Yeats on actress Mrs Patrick Campbell •646

It is greatly to Mrs Patrick Campbell's credit that, bad as the play was, her acting was worse. It was a masterpiece of failure. *George Bernard Shaw on Mrs Patrick Campbell* •647

She's such a nice woman. If you knew her you'd even admire her acting.

*Mrs Patrick Campell on a fellow actress; recorded in James Agate's **diary** 6 May 1937* •648

Such a clever actress. Pity she does her hair with Bovril.

Mrs Patrick Campbell on a rival actress; in **Ned Sherrin in his Anecdotage** *(1993); attrib.* •649

All through the five acts... he played the King as though under momentary apprehension that someone else was about to play the Ace.

*Eugene Field, reviewing Creston Clarke's **King Lear**, Denver Tribune, 1880* •650

I'm amazed he was such a good shot.

*Noël Coward, on hearing that his accountant had blown his brains out;
in* **Ned Sherrin's Theatrical Anecdotes** *(1991)* •651

A woman whose face looked as if it had been
made of sugar and someone had licked it.
George Bernard Shaw on Isadora Duncan •652

Tranquilized benevolence cascading from a great height, like royalty opening a bazaar.

Kenneth Tynan on Edith Evans in **All's Well That Ends Well**, *1959* •653

I have been looking around for an appropriate
wooden gift and am pleased hereby to present you
with Elsie Ferguson's performance in her new play.

Alexander Woollcott sends a congratulatory telegram for
George S. Kaufman's fifth wedding anniversary;
Howard Teichmann, George S. Kaufman *(1973)* •654

With his full mane of curly hair and
dressed in a gold-encrusted tightly
fitting mini-skirted costume, he
struck me as more of an overweight
elf than the savage conqueror of Asia.

Arthur Thirkell on Albert Finney in Tamberlaine, *1976* •655

Finney's roughneck Hamlet is no prince at all,
let alone a sweet prince. More of a Spamlet really.

Jason Hillgate on Albert Finney's performance at the Old Vic, 1975. In Theatre •656

One critic complained
that I had only two
gestures — left hand up,
and right hand down.
What did he expect me to
do? Bring out my prick?

John Gielgud •657

Lillian Gish may be a
charming person, but she
is not Ophelia. She comes
on stage as if she had been
sent for to sew rings
on the new curtains.

Mrs Patrick Campbell; in
Margot Peters, Mrs Pat *(1984)* •658

Farley Granger played
Mr. Darcy with all
the flexibility of a
telegraph pole.

Brooks Atkins, on Bo Goldman's musical
adaptation of Pride and Prejudice *on*
Broadway in the 1950s •659

Very good, very good.
I always thought you
would make an impression
on the stage one day.

Sir William Schewnk Gilbert, to prima
donna actress Henrietta Hodson, after she
sat down and missed the chair. •660

Mrs Holden acting his wife entered in a hurry crying
"Oh my dear Count.' She inadvertently left out the 'o'
in the pronunciation of the word count, giving it a
vehement accent, put the house into such a laughter
that London Bridge at low tide was silence to it.

An early review (1708) of Mrs Holden as
Lady Capulet in **Romeo and Juliet** •661

If they'd stuffed the child's head up the horse's arse,
they would have solved two problems at once.
Noël Coward, referring to a performance starring child actress
Bonnie Langford and a horse after the latter defecated on stage •662

Geraldine McEwan, powdered white like a clownish,
whey-faced doll simpered, whined and groaned to
such effect as the Queen, that Edward's homosexuality
became both understandable and forgivable.
Milton Shulman on a production of Brecht's **Edward II** •663

Anna Neagle playing Queen Victoria always made me think that Albert must have married beneath him.

Noël Coward, in Sheridan Morley, **The Quotable Noël Coward** *(1999)* •664

He delivers every line with a monotonous tenor bark as if addressing an audience of deaf Eskimos… It was P.G. Wodehouse who memorably said that the 'Tomorrow and tomorrow and tomorrow' speech has got a lot of spin on it but, as delivered by Mr. O'Toole, it is hit for six like a full toss.

Michael Billington reviews Peter O'Toole as **Macbeth** *in 1980 in* **The Guardian** •665

Denis Quilley played the role with all the charm
and animation of the leg of a billiard table.
Bernard Levin on Denis Quilley as Charles Condamine in
High Spirits *(a musical version of Noël Coward's* **Blithe Spirit)** •666

He has taken to ambling across our stages,
in a special, shell-shocked manner, choosing
odd moments to jump and frisk, like a man
through whom an electric current is being
intermittently passed. *Kenneth Tynan on Ralph
Richardson in* **The White
Carnation** *by R.C. Sheriff* •667

Ralph Richardson's Uncle Vanya
is just his Falstaff with a hangover.
George Jean Nathan, US critic, 1946 •668

Diana Rigg is built like a brick mausoleum
with insufficient flying buttresses.
*John Simon reviews Diana Rigg in a 1970
production of* **Abelard and Heloise;** *in*
Diana Rigg, No Turn Unstoned *(1982)* •669

She was so dramatic she stabbed the potatoes at dinner.
Sydney Smith enhances actress Sarah Siddons' reputation for melodrama •670

Mr. Torn allows words to revolve wanly in his mouth like a jingling key chain in a bored man's pocket.

John Simon on Rip Torn's performance in **Daughter of Silence; Music Box,** *November 1961* •671

Do you know how they are going to decide the Shakespeare-Bacon dispute? They are going to dig up Shakespeare and dig up Bacon; they are going to set their coffins side by side, and then they are going to get Tree to recite Hamlet to them and the one who turns in his coffin will be the author of the play.

W.S. Gilbert on actor Sir Herbert Beerbohm Tree •672

There is no point in seeing a man reduced to hysterical panic if hysterical panic is his forte.

Michael Billington on Kenneth Williams in the farce, **Signed and Sealed** •673

As swashbuckling Cyrano, Mr Woodward's performance buckles more often than it swashes.

Kenneth Hurren, **The Spectator,** *1970* •674

He is an old bore. Even the grave yawns for him.

Herbert Beerbohm Tree, of actor Israel Zangwill; in Max Beerbohm, **Herbert Beerbohm Tree** *(1920)* •675

The syphilis and gonorrhoea of the theatre.
David Mamet on Frank Rich and John Simon, critics •676

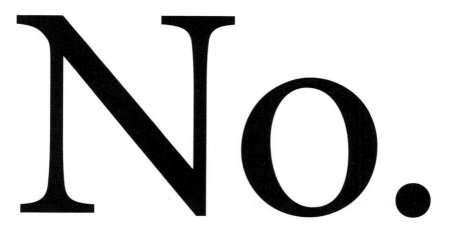

Review in a London newspaper of A Good Time, *a show running at the Duchess Theatre in the early 1900s* •677

He gives the impression that he is a Rotarian pork butcher about to tell the stalls a dirty story.

Felix Barker on Anthony Hopkins as Macbeth, 1973 •678

This is the kind of show that gives pornography a bad name.

Clive Barnes on Oh Calcutta!, *1969* •679

The Elder Statesman is a zombie play designed for the living dead.

Alan Brien on T.S. Eliot's play; in The Spectator, *September 1958* •680

The Birthday Party is like a vintage Hitchcock thriller which has been, in the immortal tear-stained words of Orson Welles, edited by a cross-eyed studio janitor with a lawn-mower.

Alan Brien reviews Harold Pinter's play in The Spectator, *May 1958* •681

Am sitting in the smallest room of my house.
Your review is before me. In a moment, it will
be behind me. *Noël Coward, apocryphal* •682

At the beginning of *Hamlet* the stage looks like a Build-Your-Own-Elsinore kit.
Robert Cushman in the **Observer**, *1981* •683

Shut up, Arnold, or I'll direct
this play the way you wrote it!
*John Dexter, to the playwright Arnold Wesker;
in* **Ned Sherrin in his Anecdotage** *(1993)* •684

The real complexity of life among Mr. Lonsdale's powerfully sexed
grammarians can be indicated in a sentence, though a tough one:
Michael, engaged to Molly, is really in love with Diana, whom he
seduced once in Paris; George can't decide whether to marry Celia
or Maggie, both of whom he has seduced here and there at various
times; and Elsie, though married to Reggie, is still strongly attracted
to her first husband, John, who has seduced practically everybody and
likes to talk about it. Anyway, all these people, along with a drunken
butler and an old family lawyer, both standard models, are visible
on the stage, sometimes at once. *Wolcott Gibbs on* **Another Love Story**
by Frederick Lonsdale. From **Seasons in
the Sun & Other Pleasures** *(1946)* •685

"

Having decided to focus on the hole rather than the doughnut, as it were, Ensler happily disappears up it. *Germaine Greer on Eve Ensler's* **The Vagina Monologues;** *in the* **Daily Telegraph,** *March 2002* •686

I want something to keep me awake thinking it was the food I ate and not the show I saw.

George S. Kaufman after a disastrous preview; in Howard Teichmann, **George S. Kaufmann** *(1973)* •687

If a director doesn't want to do *The Shrew*, this is a pretty good way not to do it.

Stanley Kaufmann on the American Conservatory Theater's production of Shakespeare's **The Taming of the Shrew,** *December 1973* •688

There was laughter in the back of the theatre, leading to the belief that someone was telling jokes back there.

George S. Kaufman; in Howard Teichmann, **George S. Kaufman** *(1973)* •689

On its face value, it is callous and empty enough:
what lies in its Freudian depths one dreads to think.

Anthony Seymour on Pinter's **The Homecoming,** *in the* **Yorkshire Post** *June 1965* •690

I think I'll go by boat.

Bernard Levin on **Boeing Boeing** *by Marc Camoletti* •691

… Its like is rarely met with except
on a fishmonger's slab, and now I feel
very ill indeed, and would like to lie down.

Bernard Levin on **The Amorous Prawn,** *1959* •692

The plot is of such titanic and recondite imbecility that I couldn't reveal it if I wanted to…

Most of the dialogue consists of members of the cast explaining the plot to one another, a service I can well imagine they need.

But I cannot see that they need the explanations to be couched in language of such shattering banality.

Bernard Levin in the **Daily Express** *on* **William Fairchild's**
The Sound of Murder, *August 1959* •693

The pitiful little thing has to do with horse racing, and you might perhaps say that it is by Imbecility out of Staggering Incompetence.

Bernard Levin on **Dazzling Prospect** *by M.J. Farrell and John Perry; in the* **Daily Express,** *June 1961* •694

I didn't like the play, but then I saw it under adverse conditions — the curtain was up.

Groucho Marx; ad-lib, attributed in an interview by Marx to George S. Kaufman; Peter Hay, Broadway Anecdotes *(1989)* •695

There are bad nights at the theater, and then once in a blue moon comes a lulu like the New Group revival of Eugene O'Neill's *Mourning Becomes Electra*, four hours of quicksand from which you begin to fear you will never, ever escape. Attending this professional production in the country's theatrical capital, you might be forgiven for imagining you were in a stuffy high school gym in an anonymous suburb, hostage to the delusional ambitions of an overweening drama teacher who really needs to go back on his medications.
Charles Isherwood in the New York Times, *2009* •696

For all its frenzied breast-beating, this is a show with about as much heart as the Tin Man in The Wizard of Oz.

Charles Osborne on West End musical Miss Saigon. *In* First Nights, Second Thoughts *(2001)* •697

All my envy goes to the inspired Mr. Walter Winchell, who walked wanly out into the foyer after the third act — there are four acts and they are long, long acts — and summed up the whole thing in the phrase, Well, for Chrichton out loud!

Dorothy Parker, in the New Yorker, *reviewing the Broadway opening of J.M. Barrie's play* The Admirable Chrichton •698

It aims at being a despairing cry but achieves only the stature of a self-pitying snivel.

Milton Shulman on John Osborne's Look Back In Anger •699

The Cigarette Girl certainly made me gasp in amazement, it is so unbelievably bad. …The dialogue is putrid, the acting early marionette, the evening disastrous. *Arthur Thirkell on* The Cigarette Girl *by William Douglas Home, 1962* •700

The play grated on me like the sustained whine of an ancient tramcar coming down a steep hill.

J.C. Trewin reviews John Osborne's Look Back in Anger *in* The London Illustrated News, *May 1956* •701

Fram is an embarrassing and indulgent piece, whose rhyming couplets, though occasionally aspiring to elegance, more often resemble pantomime doggerel. And what a dog's breakfast the play itself is.

Charles Spencer in the Daily Telegraph *on Tony Harrison's* Fram *at the National Theatre, a play my wife and I were unfortunate enough to see* •702

Miss Hunnicutt's Viola was not Patience on a Monument — it was a monument of patience.

Bernard Levin on Gayle Hunnicutt as Viola in Twelfth Night •703

When you've seen all of Ionesco's plays, I felt at the end, you've seen one of them.

Kenneth Tynan, after seeing **Victims of Duty** *by* ***Eugène Ionesco, 1960*** •704

Fredrick Leighton: My dear Mr Whistler, you leave your pictures in such a sketchy, unfinished state. Why don't you ever finish them?

James Whistler: My dear Leighton, why do you ever begin yours?

•705

It resembles a tortoise-shell cat having a fit in a plate of tomatoes.

Mark Twain on J.M.W. Turner's **The Slave Ship** •706

The only genius with an IQ of 60.

Gore Vidal on Andy Warhol •707

Skill without imagination is craftsmanship and gives us many useful objects such as wickerwork picnic baskets. Imagination without skill gives us modern art.

Tom Stoppard, **Artist Descending a staircase,** *BBC Radio, 1972* •708

Jeff Koons' work is the last bit of methane left in the intestine of the dead cow that is post-modernism.

Time *magazine's Robert Hughes on sculptor Jeff Koons* •709

When I look at these works, 'culture' only makes me think of yoghurt.

Edna Weiss, Royal Academian, on the Turner Prize shortlist •710

A decorator tainted
with insanity.

*Kenyon Cox, on
Paul Gauguin* •711

Klee's pictures seem
to me to resemble,
not pictures, but
a sample book of
patterns for linoleum.

*Sir Cyril Asquith, in a letters to Alfred
Munnings, President of the Royal Academy
at the time* •713

M Cezanne gives the
impression of being a
sort of madman who
paints in fits of
delirium tremens.

Marc de Montifond •712

Like a carbuncle on the face
of any old and valued friend.

*Charles, Prince of Wales, 1986,
on a proposed extension to
the National Gallery* •714

A critic is a person who will slit the throat of a skylark to see what makes it sing.

J.M. Synge •715

Asking a playwright how he felt about critics was like asking a lamppost how it felt about dogs.

Christopher Hampton, in **The Times** *April 1995* •716

Critics are like eunuchs in a harem; they know how it's done, they've seen it done every day, but they're unable to do it themselves.

Brendan Behan •717

I never read a book before reviewing it — it prejudices a man so.

Sydney Smith (1771-1845), clergyman and wit •718

A louse in the locks of literature.

Alfred, Lord Tennyson isn't a fan of critic John Churton Collins; in Evan Charteris, 'Life and Letters of Sir Edmund Gosse' *(1931)* •719

After all, one knows one's weak points so well, that it's rather bewildering to have the critics overlook them and invent others.

Edith Wharton, letter, 19 November 1909 •720

A critic is a man who knows the way but can't drive the car.
Kenneth Tynan, in **New York Times Magazine** *9 January 1966* •721

> There is, perhaps, no more dangerous man in the world
> than the man with the sensibilities of an artist but without
> creative talent. With luck such men make wonderful theatrical
> impresarios and interior decorators, or else they become mass
> murderers or critics. *Barry Humphries,* **More Please** *(1992)* •722

> > Thou eunuch of language… thou pimp
> > of gender… murderous accoucheur of
> > infant learning… thou pickle-herring
> > in the puppet show of nonsense.
> > *Scots poet Robert Burns on an anonymous critic* •723

Last night I dined out in Chelsea, and mauled the dead and rotten
carcases of several works written by my friends. *Virginia Woolf* •724

> Your critic has cleared himself of the charge of personal
> malice… but he has only done so by a tacit admission that
> he has really no critical instinct about literature and literary
> work, which, in one who writes about literature, is, I need
> hardly say, a much graver fault than malice of any kind.
> *Oscar Wilde,* **In Defence of Dorian Gray** *(1891)* •725

An editor is one who separates the wheat from the chaff and prints the chaff.

Adlai Stevenson, **The Stevenson Wit** *(1966)* •726

Some of the editors wrote rejection slips that were more creative than anything I had written. On my tenth submission to Redbook…
"Mrs Clark, your stories are light, slight, and trite." My first novella was returned with the succinct note: "We found the heroine as boring as her husband had."

Mary Higgins Clark, in **The Writing Life: Collection** *from* **Washington Post Book World** *(2003)* •727

Scribbler, n. A professional writer whose views are antagonistic to one's own.

Ambrose Bierce, **The Devil's Dictionary** *(1911)* •728

The media. It sounds like a convention of spiritualists.

Tom Stoppard •729

The fact that a man is a newspaper reporter is evidence of some flaw of character.

Lyndon B Johnson •730

Lickspittle, n.
A useful functionary,
not infrequently found
editing a newspaper...
Ambrose Bierce, The Devil's Dictionary
(1911) •731

There is nothing at all
the matter with some
journalists that a quick
slap in the face couldn't
sort out. *Elvis Costello (1995)* •732

David Frost has
risen without a trace.

*Kitty Muggeridge on journalist and
interviewer David Frost; in conversation
with Malcolm Muggeridge c. 1965* •733

So boring you fall asleep
halfway through her name.
*Alan Bennett on Arianna Stassinopoulos
(now Arianna Huffington) in the* Observer •734

A one-man slum.
*An anonymous commentator on American
journalist Heywood Broun (1888-1939)* •735

217

Muggeridge, a garden gnome expelled from Eden, has come to rest as a gargoyle brooding over a derelict cathedral.
Kenneth Tynan on Malcolm Muggeridge •736

A legend in his own lunchtime.
David Climie, of Dennis Main Wilson; also attrib. to Christopher Wordsworth of Clifford Makins •738

I cannot take seriously the criticism of someone who doesn't know how to use a semi-colon.

Shirley Conran on Julie Burchill •737

Books are not made like children but like pyramids... and they're just as useless! And they stay in the desert!... Jackals piss at their feet and the bourgeois climb up on them.
Gustave Flaubert, **letter to** **Ernest Feydeau,** *1857* •739

There are books of which the backs and covers are by far the best parts.

Charles Dickens •740

The more I read him, the less
I wonder that they poisoned him.
Lord Macaulay on Socrates •741

Plato is a bore.

Friedrich Nietzsche •742

A Methodist parson in Bedlam.

Horace Walpole on Dante •743

The swish-swash of the press,
the bum of impudency, the
shambles of beastliness…
the toadstool of the realm.

*Gabriel Harvey on 16th Century pamphleteer
and playwright Thomas Nashe* •744

This dodipoule, this didpopper… why, thou
arrant butter whoe, thou coteueane and
scrattop of scoldes, will thou never leave
affecting a dead Carcasse… a wispe, a wispe,
rippe, rippe, you kitchen-stuff wrangler!

Thomas Nashe, on Gabriel Harvey •745

With the single exception of Homer, there is no eminent writer, not even Sir Walter Scott, whom I can despise so entirely as I despise Shakespeare when I measure my mind against his.

George Bernard Shaw in **Saturday Review**
September 1896 •746

Having never had any mental vision, he has now lost his bodily sight; a silly coxcomb, fancying himself a beauty; an unclean beast, with nothing more human about him than his guttering eyelids; the fittest doom for him would be to hang him on the highest gallows, and set his head on the Tower of London.

Salmasius (Claude de Saumaise)
on blind poet John Milton •747

This obscure, this eccentric and disgusting poem.

Voltaire, on John Milton's epic poem
Paradise Lost •748

Doth that lewd harlot,
  that poetic queen,
Famed through White Friars,
  you know who I mean,
Mend for reproof, others set
  up in spight,
To flux, take glisters, vomits,
  purge and write.
Long with a sciatica she's
  beside lame,
Her limbs distortured,
  nerves shrunk up with pain,
And therefore I'll all sharp
  reflections shun,
Poverty, poetry, pox are plagues
  enough for one.

Anonymous, The Epistle of Julian
*(published 1687), referring to Restoration
playwright Aphra Behn* •749

It is a pretty poem, Mr Pope,
but you must not call it Homer.

*Richard Bentley, when pressed by Pope
to comment on* 'My Homer', *i.e. Pope's
translation of the* Iliad. In John Hawkins (ed.),
The Works of Samuel Johnson *(1787)* •750

A monster gibbering
shrieks, and gnashing
imprecations against
mankind — tearing
down all shreds of
modesty, past all
sense of manliness and
shame; filthy in word,
filthy in thought, furious,
raging, obscene.

*William Makepeace Thackeray
on Jonathan Swift, author of*
Gulliver's Travels •751

I do not think this poem
will reach its destination.
Voltaire on Jean-Baptiste Rousseau's
Ode To Posterity •752

I'm glad you'll write,
You'll furnish paper when I shite.
Lady Mary Wortley Montagu (1689-1762),
'Reasons that Induced Dr S- to write a Poem
called the **'Lady's Dressing Room'** •753

Thomas Gray walks
as if he had fouled
his small-clothes, and
looks as if he smelt it.
Christopher Smart, of fellow poet
Thomas Gray •754

Gibbon's style is detestable,
but it is not the worst thing
about him. *Samuel Taylor Coleridge*
on Edward Gibbon •755

Very nice, though
there are dull stretches.
Antoine de Rivarol on a two-line poem •756

A philosophising servant…
that hyena in petticoats.
Horace Walpole on Mary Wollstonecraft,
Letters, *1798* •757

It is long yet vigorous,
like the penis of a jackass.

Sydney Smith on an article in the
Edinburgh Review *by Henry Brougham* •760

How thankful we ought to be
that Wordsworth was only a
poet and not a musician. Fancy
a symphony by Wordsworth!
Fancy having to sit it out! And
fancy what it would have been
if he had written fugues!

Samuel Butler (1835-1902),
Notebooks *(1912)* •758

What a hideous,
odd-looking man
Sydney Smith is.
With a mouth like
an oyster and three
double chins

Mrs Brookfield, on the
Reverend Sydney Smith •761

An Archangel
a little damaged.

Charles Lamb on Samuel Taylor Coleridge,
letter to Wordsworth, *26 April 1816* •759

> On Waterloo's ensanguined plain
> Full many a gallant man was slain,
> But none, by sabre or by shot,
> Fell half so flat as Walter Scott.

Anonymous, of Scott's poem
'The Field of Waterloo' *(1815)* •762

It seems a great pity that they allowed her to die a natural death.

Mark Twain's apocryphal assessment of Jane Austen •763

The Edinburgh praises Jack Keats or Ketch or whatever
his names are; — why his is the Onanism of poetry.
Lord Byron finds a self-indulgent streak in the work of fellow poet John Keats;
in a letter to his publisher John Murray, 4 November 1820 •764

> I see a schoolboy when I think of him
> With face and nose pressed to a sweet-shop window,
> For certainly he sank into his grave
> His senses and his heart unsatisfied,
> And made — being poor, ailing and ignorant,
> Shut out from all the luxury of the world,
> The ill-bred son of a livery stable-keeper-
> Luxuriant song.

W.B. Yeats qualifies his praise of Keats,
'Ego Dominus Tuus' *(1917)* •765

Always looking at himself in mirrors to make sure he was sufficiently outrageous.
Enoch Powell on Lord Byron, **Sunday Times** *May 1988* •766

I never heard a single expression of fondness for him fall from the lips of any of those who knew him well. *Lord Macaulay on Lord Byron,* **letter** *7 June 1831* •767

Mad, bad, and dangerous to know.
Lady Charles Lamb's assessment, in her diary, of Lord Byron after their first meeting at a ball in March 1812 •768

The world is rid of Lord Bryon, but the deadly slime of his touch still remains.
John Constable, artist, on news of Byron's death •769

He is a person of very epic appearance — and has a fine head as far as the outside goes — and wants nothing but taste to make the inside equally attractive.
Lord Byron, *of poet and writer Robert Southey;* letter, *30 September 1813* •770

Mr. Southey wades through the ponderous volumes of travels and old chronicles, from which he carefully selects all that is false, useless and absurd, as being essentially poetical; and when he has a commonplace book full of monstrosities, strings them into an epic.
Thomas Love Peacock on the British poet laureate Robert Southey,
***in* The Four Ages of Poetry, *(1820)* •771**

Our opinion then is this: that Barère approached
nearer than any person mentioned in history or fiction,
whether man or devil, to the idea of consummate and
universal depravity. In him the qualities which are the
proper objects of contempt, preserve an exquisite and
absolute harmony. When we put everything together,
sensuality, poltroonery, baseness, effrontery, mendacity,
barbarity, the result is something which in a novel
we should condemn as caricature, and to which,
we venture to say, no parallel can be found in history.
Thomas Babington, Lord Macaulay, reviewing the memoirs of
French revolutionary Bertrand Barère, in a passage once described
as the most sustained piece of invective in the English language •772

A great cow full of ink.
Gustave Flaubert on George Sand •773

At bottom, this Macaulay is but a poor creature with his
dictionary literature and erudition, his saloon arrogance.
He has no vision in him. He will neither see nor do anything great.
Thomas Carlyle on Thomas Babington Macaulay •774

I wish her characters would talk a little less
like the heroes and heroines of police reports.
George Eliot, on Jane Eyre *by Charlotte Brontë* •775

227

A dirty man with opium-glazed eyes and rat-taily hair.

Lady Frederick Cavendish on Alfred, Lord Tennyson •776

He could not think up to the height of his own towering style.

G.K. Chesterton on Alfred, Lord Tennyson; The Victorian Age in Literature *(1912)* •777

Longfellow is to poetry what the barrel-organ is to music.

Van Wyck Brooks on Henry Wadsworth Longfellow •778

A large shaggy dog unchained scouring the beaches of the world and baying at the moon. *Robert Louis Stevenson on Walt Whitman* •779

I could readily see in Emerson… a gaping flaw. It was the insinuation that had he lived in those days when the world was made, he might have offered some valuable suggestions.

*Herman Melville on
Ralph Waldo Emerson* •780

Arnold is a dandy Isaiah, a poet without passion, whose verse, written in surplice, is for freshmen and for gentle maidens who will be wooed to the arms of these future rectors.

*George Meredith on the poet
and essayist Matthew Arnold,
in* Fortnightly Review
July 1909 •781

Carlyle is a poet to whom nature has denied the faculty of verse.

Alfred, Lord Tennyson, **letter to W.E. Gladstone,** *c.1870* •782

It was very good of God to let Carlyle and Mrs Carlyle marry one another and so make only two people miserable instead of four.
Samuel Butler, **letter to Miss E.M.A. Savage,** *21 November 1884* •783

The same old sausage, fizzing and sputtering in its own grease.
Henry James on Thomas Carlyle •784

I was never allowed to read the popular American children's books of my day because, as my mother said, the children spoke bad English without the author's knowing it. *Edith Wharton* •785

The original Greek is of great use in elucidating Browning's translation of the Agamemnon.

Robert Yelverton Tyrell's habitual remark to students; in Ulick O'Connor, Oliver St John Gogarty *(1964)* •786

A provincial manufacturer of gauche and heavy fictions that sometimes have corresponding values.

Critic F.R. Leavis on Thomas Hardy •787

No one has written worse English than Mr. Hardy in some of his novels — cumbrous, stilted, ugly, and inexpressive. *Virginia Woolf on Thomas Hardy,* **The Moment,** *(1947)* •788

A little emasculated mass of inanity.

Theodore Roosevelt on Henry James •789

Henry James has a mind so fine no idea could violate it. *T.S. Eliot* •790

> The work of Henry James has always seemed divisible by a simple dynastic arrangement into three reigns: James I, James II, and the Old Pretender.
>
> *Philip Guadella,* Collected Essay, 'Men of Letters: Mr Henry James' *(1920)* •791

The scratching of pimples on the body of the bootboy at Claridge's.
Virginia Woolf's assessment of James Joyce's Ulysses, in a letter of 1922 •792

> I am reading Henry James…
> and feel myself as one entombed
> in a block of smooth amber.
>
> *Virginia Woolf on Henry James* •793

She plunged into a sea of platitudes, and with the powerful breast stroke of a channel swimmer made her way towards the white cliffs of the obvious.

W. Somerset Maugham on Virginia Woolf •794

Concerning no subject would Shaw be deterred by the minor accident of total ignorance from penning a definitive opinion.

Roger Scruton on George Bernard Shaw •795

On remarking that George Bernard Shaw's wife was a good listener: God knows she's had plenty of practice.

J.B. Priestley, Margin Released *(1962)* •796

Silence — the most perfect expression of scorn. *George Bernard Shaw,* **Back to Methuselah,** *(1921).* *If only he'd taken his own advice* •797

When you were a little boy somebody ought to have said hush just once.

Mrs Patrick Campbell, **letter to George Bernard Shaw,** *1 November 1912* •798

> Hugo — hélas!
> (Hugo — alas!)

*André Gide, when asked who was the
greatest 19th-century poet. In Claude Martin,*
La Maturité d'André Gide *(1977)* •799

The human race, to which so
many of my readers belong.

G. K. Chesterton •800

Conrad spent a day finding
the mot juste; then killed it.

Ford Madox Ford, in Robert Lowell, Notebook 1967-68 *(1969)* •801

What is Conrad but the
wreck of Stevenson floating
about in the slipslop of
Henry James. *George Moore on the
novelist Joseph Conrad.* •802

A jingo imperialist, morally insensitive and aesthetically disgusting.
George Orwell on Rudyard Kipling •803

I have always thought it was a sound
impulse by which he [Kipling] was
driven to put his 'Recessional' into
the waste-paper basket, and a great
pity that Mrs Kipling fished it out
and made him send it to *The Times*.
Max Beerbohm, letter, *30 October 1913* •804

As a contribution to natural history the work is negligible.
E.V. Lucas in a review of Kenneth Grahame's Wind in the Willows;
in Times Literary Supplement *22 October 1908* •805

I am also writing a preface for an American edition
of Galsworthy's Man of Property. Ever read it?
Don't. He was the last English novelist to be granted
general reverence. He is really shockingly dull.
I had the hope that it was youthful snobbery that
made me despise him. But no. He's no good.
Evelyn Waugh, in a letter to Anne Fleming, *7 August 1963.*
From The Letters of Evelyn Waugh *(1980)* •806

> E.M. Forster never gets any further than warming the teapot. He's a rare fine hand at that. Feel this teapot. Is it not beautifully warm? Yes, but there ain't going to be no tea. *Katherine Mansfield on E.M. Forster,* **diary entry,** *May 1917* •807

He is limp and damp and milder than the breath of a cow.

Virginia Woolf on E.M. Forster •808

A village explainer, excellent if you were a village, but if you were not, not. *Gertrude Stein on Ezra Pound* •809

How unpleasant to meet Mr Eliot!
With his features of clerical cut,
And his brow so grim
And his mouth so prim
And his conversation, so nicely
Restricted to What Precisely
And If and Perhaps and But.

A particularly caustic (but not totally inaccurate) self-assessment from T.S. Eliot, 'Five-Finger Exercises' (1936) •810

Self-contempt, well-grounded.

F.R. Leavis (1895-1978) on the foundation of T.S. Eliot's work, in Times Literary Supplement *21 October 1988* •811

A bestseller is the gilded tomb of a mediocre talent.
Logan Pearsall Smith, **Afterthoughts** *(1931)* •812

I am fairly unrepentant about the poetry. I really think that
three quarters of it is gibberish. However, I must crush down
these thoughts, otherwise the dove of peace will shit on me.
Noël Coward on Dame Edith Sitwell •813

So you've been reviewing Sitwell's
last piece of Virgin dung, have you?
Isn't she a poisonous thing of a woman,
lying, concealing, flipping, plagiarising,
misquoting, and being as clever a
crooked literary publicist as ever.
Dylan Thomas on Edith Sitwell •814

The Sitwells belong to the history
of publicity rather than poetry.

FR Leavis in **New Bearings**
In English Poetry *(1932)* •815

> I am reading Proust for the first time. Very poor stuff. I think he was mentally defective.

Evelyn Waugh on Marcel Proust, in **a letter to John Betjemn,** *1948;*
in **Letters of Evelyn Waugh** *(1980)* •816

Miss Stein sometimes takes time from praising Miss Stein to drop names. Vast quantities of names. It's name-dropping because she rarely has anything worthwhile to say about the people attached to them, although they were often the people that did make a difference. **Good-Books-Bad-Books.com** *on* **Gertrude Stein's** **The Autobiography of Alice B.Toklas** •817

I am only one, only one, only one. Only one being, one at the same time. Not two, not three, only one. Only one life to live, only sixty minutes in one hour. Only one pair of eyes. Only one brain. Only one being. Being only one, having only one pair of eyes, having only one time, having only one life, I cannot read your MS three or four times. Not even one time. Only one look, only one look is enough. Hardly one copy would sell here. Hardly one. Hardly one. Many thanks. I am returning the MS by registered post. Only one MS by one post.

Rejection letter from editor A.J. Fifield to Gertrude Stein, who was renowned
(or notorious) for her uniquely repetitive style •818

Lady Chatterley's Lover — Mr Lawrence
has a diseased mind. He is obsessed by sex
and we have no doubt that he will be ostracised
by all except the most degenerate coteries
of the world. John Bull *magazine, 1928* •819

Mr Lawrence looked like a plaster gnome on a stone
toadstool in some suburban garden… he looked as
if he had just returned from spending an uncomfortable
night in a very dark cave. *Dame Edith Sitwell,*
on D.H. Lawrence •820

He has never been known to
use a word that might send
a reader to the dictionary.

William Faulkner on Ernest Hemingway •821

Poor Faulkner. Does he really think
big emotions come from big words?

Ernest Hemingway on William Faulkner •822

[*The Sun Also Rises* is about]
bullfighting, bullslinging, and bullshit.

*Zelda Fitzgerald offers a summary of Ernest Hemingway's
novel; in Marion Meade,* What Fresh Hell Is This? *(1988)* •823

English literature's performing flea.

Sean O'Casey on P.G. Wodehouse •824

His style has the desperate jauntiness
of an orchestra fiddling away for dear
life on a sinking ship. *Edmund Wilson on*
Evelyn Waugh •825

Virginia Woolf's writing is no more than
glamorous knitting. I believe she must have
a pattern somewhere. *Dame Edith Sitwell* •826

Everything he touches smells like a billygoat.
He is every kind of a writer I detest, a faux naif,
a Proust in greasy overalls. *Raymond Chandler on*
James M. Cain •827

Personally, I would rather have written Winnie-the-Pooh
than the collected works of Brecht.
Tom Stoppard, attrib. 1972 •828

The high-water mark, so to speak,
of Socialist literature is W.H. Auden,
a sort of gutless Kipling.
George Orwell, **The Road to Wigan Pier** *(1937)* •829

241

He is not really a writer, but a non-stop talker to whom someone has given a typewriter.

Gerald Brenan on Henry Miller; in Thoughts in a Dry Season *(1978)* •830

After A.A. Milne had written a letter to the *Daily Telegraph* on the report of Wodehouse's broadcasting from Germany: My personal animosity against a writer never affects my opinion of what he writes. Nobody could be more anxious than myself, for instance, that Alan Alexander Milne should trip over a loose bootlace and break his bloody neck, yet I re-read his early stuff at regular intervals with all the old enjoyment.

P.G. Wodehouse, letter, *27 November 1945* •831

Oh really. What exactly is she reading?

*Actress Dame Edith Evans, on being told that Nancy Mitford
had been lent a villa to enable her to finish a book; attrib.* •832

The insolent little ruffian,
that crapulous lout. When
he quitted a sofa, he left
behind him a smear.

Norman Cameron on Dylan Thomas •833

To see him fumbling with our rich and delicate language is to experience all the horror of seeing a Sèvres vase in the hands of a chimpanzee.

Evelyn Waugh on Stephen Spender, in The Tablet, *May 1951* •834

He is able to turn an unplotted, unworkable manuscript into an unplotted and unworkable manuscript with a lot of sex. *Tom Volpe on Harold Robbins* •835

When it comes down to it, *Lucky Jim* is *Just William*, bigger and bespectacled, literate and funny, but scarcely grown-up.
Simon Gray on Kingsley Amis' Lucky Jim, in The Times February 1966 •836

Howl is meant to be a noun, but I can't help taking it as an imperative. *John Hollander on Howl by Allan Ginsberg in The Partisan Review* •837

No, I don't think Lolita any good except as smut. As that it was highly exciting to me.
Evelyn Waugh on Vladimir Nabokov's Lolita, in a letter to Nancy Mitford, 29 June 1959; in Letters of Evelyn Waugh (1980) •838

The trouble with Ian Fleming is that he gets off with women because he can't get on with them.

English novelist Rosamund Lehmann borrows a line from Elizabeth Bowen in her assessment of the James Bond author; in J. Pearson, The Life of Ian Fleming *(1966)* •839

Good career move.

Gore Vidal, of Truman Capote's death; attrib. •840

A man who so much resembled a Baked Alaska — sweet, warm and gungy on the outside, hard and cold within. *Francis King, of English novelist and scientist C.P. Snow;* Yesterday Came Suddenly *(1993)* •841

I would rather read a novel about civil servants written by a rabbit.

Craig Brown, on hearing that Richard Adams' Watership Down *was a novel about rabbits written by a civil servant; attrib.* •842

This is one of those big, fat paperbacks,
intended to while away a monsoon or two,
which, if thrown with a good over-arm action,
will bring a water buffalo to its knees.

Nancy Banks-Smith, review of M.M. Kaye's The Far Pavilions •843

Ms. Greer's most succinct descriptive writing is in the title
of her book, which characterises the text with precision.

Brigid Brophy on Germaine Greer's The Obstacle Race;
in London Review of Books, *November 1979* •844

To a Hollywood writer who had criticised the work of Alan Bennett: Listen, dear, you couldn't write fuck on a dusty venetian blind.

English actress Coral Browne; attib., in Sunday Times Magazine *1984* •845

He was not a serious politician.
But his footwork should command
respect. He is proof of the proposition
that in each of us lurks one bad novel.

Julian Critchley on Jeffrey Archer •846

The meringue-utan.

Maurice Bowra (1898-1971), of author Rosamund Lehmann, in The Spectator *July 1999* •847

I am as shallow as a puddle.

Helen Fielding, creator of **Bridget Jones** •848

"

The covers of this book are too far apart.

Ambrose Bierce, review •849

Heaven sends us good meat,
but the Devil sends cooks.

David Garrick, On Doctor Goldsmith's Characteristical Cookery *(1777)* •850

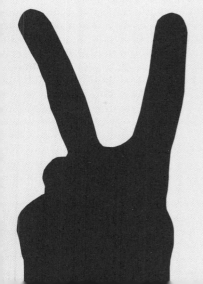

They make a rare soop they call Pepper-Pot; it's an excellent Breakfast for a Salamander, or a good preparative for a Mountebank's Agent, who Eats Fire one day, that he may get better Victual the next. Three Spoonfuls so Inflam'd my Mouth, that had I devoured a Peck of Horse-Radish, and Drank after it a Gallon of Brandy and Gunpowder, I could not have been more importunate for a Drop of Water to cool my Tongue. *Edward Ward* •851

When I ask for a watercress sandwich, I do not mean a loaf with a field in the middle of it. *Oscar Wilde to a waiter, recorded by Max Beerbohm in a* **letter to Reggie Turner,** *4 February 2002* •852

There are twenty ways of cooking a potato, and three hundred and sixty-four ways of cooking an egg, yet the British cook up to the present moment knows only three methods of sending up either one or the other.
Oscar Wilde, **'Dinners and Dishes'** *(1885)* •853

The average cooking in the average English hotel for the average Englishman explains to a large extent the English bleakness and taciturnity. Nobody can beam and warble while chewing pressed beef smeared with diabolical mustard. Nobody can exult aloud while ungluing from his teeth a quivering tapioca pudding. *Karel Capek* •854

Nothing but joints, joints, joints; sometimes, perhaps, a meat-pie, which, if you eat it, weighs upon your conscience, with the idea that you have eaten the scraps of other people's dinners. *Nathaniel Hawthorne on food served in English hotels* •855

The food we ate was risibly bad, the atmosphere smilingly inhospitable, the décor a sordid cliché of rural nostalgia, puppy porn and green-welly fascism — and they charge you two quid to sit on the ground outside. It is not just everything I despise and loath in lunch, but everything that embarrasses and depresses me about tweedy Albion. *The Bell at Sapperton in Gloucestershire gets the AA Gill treatment* •856

Her cooking is the missionary position of cooking. That is how everybody starts.

*Egon Ronay defends Delia Smith (and damns her with faint praise?);
in* **Independent on Sunday,** *November 1998* •857

Anchovies: I met my first anchovy on a pizza in 1962, and it was seven years before I mustered the courage to go near another. I am known to cross a street whenever I see an anchovy coming. Why would anybody consciously choose to eat a tiny, oil-soaked, leathery maroon strip of rank and briny flesh
Jeffrey Steingarten on **My food phobias,** *in his introduction to*
The Man Who Ate Everything *(1997)* •858

The anchovy starter was the worst thing I've eaten since I inadvertently swallowed a large flying insect while laughing open-mouthed in Greece. *Sue Townsend* •859

"Mass-produced food, poor service, and a cold atmosphere — brickbats abound for the cavernous relaunched Liverpool Street hotel dining room which has London's leading restaurant name behind it — Conran crap at Conran prices, as one reviewer succinctly put it.
Report on Aurora, in **Harden's London Restaurants 2001** •860

Nobu-lite is taking over the eating-out world. It's not McDonald's that's the real sin of exploitative globalisation, it's this no-no-Nobu non-food. Sushi-size me? Frankly, I'd rather eat with the fishes. *AA Gill on*
Sumosan •861

The name Big Mac is generally supposed to have come about because it is a big McDonald's burger, but in fact it was named after the big raincoat whose taste it so closely resembles. *Jo Brand* •862

It was like chewing a vasectomy scar with a pustular, yellow skin — as nasty a burger as I've eaten this year.
AA Gill on the fayre at The Barnes Grill •863

Clams: I feel a mild horror about what goes on in the wet darkness between the shells of all bivalves, but clams are the only ones I dislike. Is it their rubbery consistency or their rank subterranean taste, or is the horror deeper than I know? *Jeffrey Steingarten on* **My food phobias**, *in his introduction to* **The Man Who Ate Everything** *(1997)* •864

Turbot, Sir, said the waiter, placing before me two
fishbones, two eyeballs, and a bit of a black mackintosh.
Thomas Earle Welby, in **The Dinner Knell** *(1932)* **'Birmingham or Crewe?'** •865

Adults who require a salad at every meal are like obsessed little children who will
eat nothing but frozen pizza or canned ravioli for months on end. They tuck into
the dreariest salad simply because it is raw and green. No matter that the arugula
is edged with brown, the croutons taste rancid, the vinegar burns like battery acid.
No matter that it is the dead of winter when salad chills us to the marrow and we
should be eating preserved meats and hearty roots, garbures, and cassoulet.
No matter that they are keeping me from my desert. They think nothing of
interrupting a perfectly nice meal with their superstitious salad ritual.
Jeffrey Steingarten in **The Man Who Ate Everything** *(1997)* •866

The catering trade is laughingly called the hospitality industry.
That's a joke. Any less hospitable industry would be hard to
find. The frequent receptionist greeting "Have you got a
reservation?" typifies the arrogance of many restaurants…
How many times are you greeted in a restaurant with a smile?
A smile to most restaurant employees is like a silver cross to a vampire.
Michael Winner, in his introduction to **Winner's Dinners** *(2000)* •867

Conran complacency shines through at this noisy and cavernous Soho tourist-trap;
surly service and slapdash cooking too often make it a waste of time and money.
Report on Mezzo, in **Harden's London Restaurants** *2002* •868

The food at Jaan is, by turns stupid, ill thought-out, or just plain nasty. I may not be able to call it the worst cooking in Britain, but that's only because I haven't eaten in every restaurant in the land. Why am I being so harsh? Because a meal here with wine will set you back £65 a head. You do not spend this sort of money so that chefs can do ludicrous things to food. *Jay Rayner in* **The Observer** •869

> The soup, thin and dark and utterly savourless,
> tasted as if it had been drained out of the
> umbrella stand. *Margaret Halsey on English cuisine* •870

None of Liebrandt's peculiar touches, however, prepared me for the outlandish goofiness of the desserts. The creations are mostly ethereal flans, foams, and gelées made with ingredients like Pepsi, mentholyptus, or Guinness stout. The Guinness is served in jellied form, as part of a tasteless flan made with orange water; the Pepsi is reduced down, then dripped over a kind of frothy, whiskey-flavoured zabaglione. I'm not sure either of them tasted very good, but then, that's not always the point at Papillon. Spectacle is the point, and in the end, you can't help enjoying the show. *Adam Platt on Papillon in* **New York Magazine**, *February 2002* •871

I was distracted by my friend's filet mignon sandwich. Could I trust a steakhouse that serves a flavourless cut like filet mignon as its special? Dessert answered that. A single scoop of tangerine sorbet arrived in a giant round bowl. I peered in, and it reminded me of a pebble at the bottom of a well. It made me think of what Tim Zagat, a founder of Restaurant Week, said. It's in the interest of the restaurant to do it well, he said. If the restaurant goes cheap, the restaurant is just damaging its own image. Indeed. Next time, I'll buy a hot dog and take in the view from the terminal steps. *Amanda Hesser on Michael Jordan's: The Steak House in Grand Central Terminus. In* **The New York Times**, *February 2002* •872

Duck magret, a cut which has become a cliché — and which often isn't magret (the fattened breast of a foie gras bird) but something puny in an a cup.

Jonathan Meades in the Times
Saturday Review, *March 1994* •873

The menu at the Café du Jardin translates poulet provençal as brick flattened chicken, which sounds like a terrible thing to happen to a fowl — the result of a tragic hod incident on La Canebiere, perhaps.

This is not the only solecism on show. The two doors to the street are constantly left open, causing the customer who has drawn the short seat to get up time and again to fight back the draught. The staff are on the diffident side. The tables are so cramped that intimacy could occur, Constable.

Jonathan Meades in the
Times Saturday Review,
March 1994 •874

I never liked beer. It's plebeian. It goes with dirty undershirts.
Hedy Lamarr •875

It has, with great panache, expense and devil-take-the-hind-most braggadocio, transformed itself into the most laughably hideous dining room in London. No, credit where credit's due, this is no time to be mealy-mouthed or damn with faint insult — why should only London bask in its horrendous radiance? It's the worst dining room in Britain, in Europe, the globe, the galaxy, history, eternity, ever.
AA Gill on the Dorchester Grill •876

"

Be content to remember that those who can make omelettes properly can do nothing else.

Hilaire Belloc, A Conversation with a Cat *(1931)* •877

When a gentleman is disposed to swear, it is not for any standers-by to curtail his oaths.

William Shakespeare, **Cymbeline** *(1609-10) I.vi* •878

The devil damn thee black,
thou cream-faced loon!

William Shakespeare, Macbeth, *V,iii* •879

A joyless, dismal, black, and sorrowful issue:
Here is the babe as loathsome as a toad amongst
the fairest breeders of our clime

William Shakespeare, Titus Andronicus *(1594) iV, ii* •880

What I think I utter, and spend
my malice in my breath.

William Shakespeare, Coriolanus *(1608) II.i* •881

I would thou didst itch
from head to foot and I
had the scratching of thee.

William Shakespeare, Troilus and Cressida *(1602) II.i* •882

Beatrice: I wonder that you will still be talking,
Signior Benedick: Nobody marks you. Benedick What!
  My dear Lady Disdain, are you yet living?

William Shakespeare, Much Ado About
Nothing *(1598-99) I.i* •883

I will go on the slightest errand now to the
Antipodes that you can devise to send
me on; I will fetch you a toothpicker now
from the furthest inch of Asia; bring you the
length of Prester John's foot; fetch you a hair
of the Great Cham's beard; do you any
embassage to the Pigmies, rather than hold
three words conference with this harpy.

William Shakespeare, Much Ado About Nothing *(1598-99) II.i* •884

I do desire we may be better strangers.

William Shakespeare, As You Like It *(1599) III.ii* •885

She speaks poniards, and every word stabs: if her breath were as terrible as her terminations, there were no living near her; she would infect to the north star.

William Shakespeare, **Much Ado About Nothing** *(1598-9) II.i* •886

Thou subtle, perjur'd, false, disloyal man!

William Shakespeare, **The Two Gentlemen of Verona** *(1592-3) IV.ii* •887

I do defy him, and spit at him; Call him a slanderous coward and a villain. *William Shakespeare,* **Richard II** *(1595) I.i* •888

Vile worm, thou wast o'er looked even in thy birth

William Shakespeare, **The Merry Wives Of Windsor***(1597) V.v* •889

A most notable coward, an infinite and endless liar, an hourly promise breaker, the owner of no one good quality worthy your Lordship's entertainment

William Shakespeare, **All's Well That Ends Well** *(1603-4) III.vi* •890

Poor virgin, sir, an ill-favoured thing, sir,
but mine own; a poor humour of mine, sir,
to take that that no man else will.

William Shakespeare, **As you Like It** *(1599-1600) V.iv* •891

That trunk of humours, that bolting-hutch of beastliness, that swollen parcel of dropsies, that huge bombard of sack, that stuffed cloak-bag of guts, that roasted Manningtree ox with pudding in his belly, that reverend vice, that grey iniquity, that father ruffian, that vanity in years.

William Shakespeare,
Henry IV, Part 1 *(1597) II.iv* •892

'sblood, you starvelling, you eel-skin, you dried neat's-tongue, you bull's pizzle, you stock-fish — O for breath to utter what is like thee! — you tailor's-yard, you sheath, you bow-case, you vile standing tuck!

William Shakespeare, **Henry IV, Part 1** *(1597) II.iv* •893

Thou art a traitor and a miscreant,
too good to be so and too bad to live.
William Shakespeare, Richard II *(1595) I.i* •894

'zounds, a dog, a rat, a mouse, a cat, to scratch a man to
death! A braggart, a rogue, a villain, that fights by the book
of arithmetic! *William Shakespeare,* Romeo And Juliet *(1595)III.i* •895

> O! he's as tedious
> As a tired horse, a railing wife;
> Worse than a smoky house. I had rather live
> With cheese and garlic in a windmill, far,
> Than feed on cates and have him talk to me
> In any summer-house in Christendom.
> *William Shakespeare,* Henry IV, Part 1 *(1597) III.i* •896

Away you scullion! You rampallion!
You fustilarian! I'll tickle
your catastophe!
William Shakespeare,
Henry IV, Part 2 *(1597) II.i* •897

263

" Why, he is the prince's jester: a very dull fool;
Only his gift is in devising impossible slanders:
None but libertines delight in him;
And the
Commendation is not in his wit, but in his villainy

William Shakespeare, Much Ado About Nothing *(1598-9) II.i* •898

Thou clay-brained guts, thou knotty-pated fool, thou whoreson obscene greasy tallow-catch!

William Shakespeare, Henry IV, Part 1 *(1597) II.iv* •899

Johnson: Well, we had a good talk.
Boswell: Yes, sir, you tossed and gored several persons.
Boswell's account of a post-prandial exchange between Johnson and himself •900

Nay, sir, we'll send you to him. If your presence doesn't drive a man out of his house, nothing will.

Samuel Johnson to James Boswell, discussing how to get a friend to leave London •901

Sir, there is no settling the point of precedency between a louse and a flea.

Samuel Johnson on the relative merits of two minor poets; in James Boswell, Life of Samuel Johnson *(1791)* 1783 •902

This man I thought had been a Lord among wits; but, I find, he is only a wit among Lords.

Samuel Johnson on Lord Chesterfield; in James Boswell, Life of Samuel Johnson *(1791)* 1754 •903

Sir, he was dull in company, dull in his chest, dull everywhere. He was dull in a new way, and that made many people think him great. He was a mechanical poet. *Samuel Johnson on Thomas Gray* •904

Young man: Tell me this, Sir, what would you give to be as young and sprightly as I am?

Johnson: Why, Sir, I should almost be content to be as foolish and conceited.

Samuel Johnson; in Kenneth Williams, Acid Drops *(1980)* •905

Johnson: Sir, it is a very vile country.

Mr S—: Well, Sir, God made it.

Johnson: Certainly he did, but we must remember that He made it for Scotchmen; and comparisons are odious,

Mr. S—: but God made Hell.

Samuel Johnson on Scotland •906

Oats. A grain, which in England is generally given
to horses but in Scotland supports the people.
Samuel Johnson, **Dictionary of the English Language** •907

Difficult do you call it, Sir? I wish it were impossible.

Samuel Johnson, on the performance of a celebrated violinist, in William Seward,
Supplement to the Anecdotes of Distinguished Persons *(1797)* •908

Paradise Lost is one of those books which the readers
admires, lays down and forgets to take up again. Its
perusal is a duty rather than a pleasure.
Samuel Johnson •909

I refute it thus.

*Samuel Johnson, kicking a large stone by way of refuting Bishop Berkeley's theory of the
non-existence of matter, in Boswell,* **Life of Samuel Johnson** *(1791)* **6 August 1763** •910

A fellow who makes no figure in company, and has
a mind as narrow as the neck of a vinegar cruet.
Samuel Johnson, in Boswell, **Journal of a Tour in the Hebrides** *(1785)* •911

I do not want people to be very agreeable, as it saves me the trouble of liking them a great deal.
Jane Austen, letter to her sister Cassandra, *24-6 December 1798* •912

Mrs Breton called here on Saturday. I never saw her before. She is large, ungenteel woman, with self-satisfied and would-be elegant manners.
Jane Austen, Letter to her sister Cassandra •913

A person and face, of strong, natural, sterling insignificance.
Jane Austen, Sense and Sensibility *(1811)* •914

I cannot anyhow continue to find people agreeable; I respect Mrs Chamberlayne for doing her hair well, but cannot feel a more tender sentiment. Miss Langley is like any other short girl, with a broad nose and wide mouth, fashionable dress and exposed bosom. Adam Stanhope is a gentleman-like man, but then his legs are too short and his tail too long. *Jane Austen,* Letter to her sister Cassandra •915

'My love, you contradict every body,' said his wife with her usual laugh. 'Do you know that you are quite rude?'
'I did not know I contradicted anybody in calling your mother ill-bred.' *Jane Austen*, Sense and Sensibility *(1811)* •916

Mrs Hall of Sherbourne was brought to bed yesterday of a dead child, some weeks before she expected, owing to a fright. I suppose she happened to look unawares at her husband.

Jane Austen, letter •917

Miss Debary, Susan and Sally… made their appearance, and I was as civil to them as their bad breath would allow me.

Jane Austen, letter to Cassandra, *11 June 1799* •918

It was a delightful visit; — perfect, in being much too short.

Jane Austen, Emma *(1816)* •919

It is perfectly monstrous the way people
go about nowadays, saying things against one
behind one's back that are absolutely true.
Oscar Wilde, **The Picture of Dorian Gray** *(1891)* •920

He hasn't an enemy in the world,
and none of his friends like him.
Oscar Wilde on George Bernard Shaw •921

One must have a heart of stone to read
the death of Little Nell without laughing.
Oscar Wilde on Charles Dickens' **Little Dorrit** •922

Mr. Henry James writes fiction
as if it were a painful duty.
Oscar Wilde •923

I hate vulgar realism in literature. The man who
would call a spade a spade should be compelled
to use one. It is the only thing he is fit for.
Oscar Wilde, **The Picture of Dorian Gray** *(1891)* •924

Gwendolen: I had no idea there were any flowers in the country.
Cecily: Oh, flowers are as common here, Miss Fairfax, as people
are in London. *Oscar Wilde,* The Importance of Being Earnest *(1895)* Act III •925

Miss Prism: No married man is ever attractive except to his wife.
Chasuble: And often, I've been told, not even to her.
Oscar Wilde, The Importance of Being Earnest *(1895)* Act II •926

…Lady Ruxton, an overdressed woman of forty-seven, with
a hooked nose, who was always trying to get herself compromised,
but was so peculiarly plain that to her great disappointment
no one would ever believe anything against her.
Oscar Wilde, The Picture of Dorian Gray *(1891)* •927

Thy body is hideous. It is like the body of a leper.
It is like a plastered wall where vipers have crawled.
Oscar Wilde, Salomé *(1894)* •928

…A dowdy girl, with one of those
characteristic British faces, that,
once seen are never remembered.
Oscar Wilde, The Picture of Dorian Gray *(1891)* •929

And now you must run away, for I am dining with some very dull people, who won't talk scandal, and I know that if I don't get my sleep now I shall never be able to keep awake during dinner.

Oscar Wilde, **Lord Arthur Savile's Crime** *(1891)* •930

Unable to accept due to a subsequent engagement.

Oscar Wilde responds to a dinner invitation; attrib., perhaps apocryphal, in Kenneth Williams, **Acid Drops** *(1980)* •931

Relations are simply a tedious pack of people, who haven't got the remotest knowledge of how to live, nor the smallest instinct about when to die.

Oscar Wilde, **The Importance of Being Earnest** *(1895)* **Act I** •932

Of course, America had been discovered before Columbus, but it had always been hushed up.

Oscar Wilde •933

It is absurd to say that there are neither ruins nor curiosities in America when they have their mothers and their manners.

Oscar Wilde •934

Wilde: How I wish I had said that.
James McNeill Whistler: You will, Oscar, you will. *In R. Ellman,* **Oscar Wilde** *(1987)* •935

Under certain circumstances, profanity provides a relief denied even to prayer. *Mark Twain* •936

Better to keep your mouth shut and appear stupid than to open it and remove all doubt.

Mark Twain; James Munson (ed.) The Sayings of Mark Twain (1992); attrib., perhaps apocryphal. Twain's advice was later dispensed by Norman Tebbit to Dennis Skinner •937

A solemn, unsmiling, sanctimonious old iceberg that looked like he was waiting for a vacancy on the Trinity.

Mark Twain, of a California leader in the 1860s, later taken up by H.L. Mencken and applied to Woodrow Wilson; in Alex Ayres (ed.), The Wit and Wisdom of Mark Twain (2005) •938

Suppose you were an idiot. And suppose you were a member of Congress. But I repeat myself.

Mark Twain; in Alex Ayres (ed.), The Wit and Wisdom of Mark Twain (2005) •939

Let his vices be forgotten and his virtues remembered; it will not infringe much upon any man's time.

Mark Twain; in Alex Ayres (ed.), The Wit and Wisdom of Mark Twain (2005) •940

I refused to attend his funeral, but I wrote a very nice letter explaining that I approved of it. *Mark Twain, on hearing of the death of a corrupt politician; in James Munson (ed.) The Sayings of Mark Twain (1992)* •941

That woman speaks eighteen langauges, and can't say 'No' in any of them.

Dorothy Parker; in Alexander Woollcott, **While Rome Burns** *(1934)* •942

If all the girls attending it were laid end to end, I wouldn't be at all surprised.

Dorothy Parker, of the Yale Prom, recalled in Alexander Woollcott, **While Rome Burns** *(1934)* •943

You can lead a horticulture, but you can't make her think.

Dorothy Parker •944

Clare Booth Luce (meeting Dorothy Parker in a doorway): Age before beauty.
Parker (proceeding through the doorway): Pearls before swine.
In R.E. Drennan, **Wit's End** *(1973)* •945

And where does she find them?

Dorothy Parker, on hearing that Clare Booth Luce was always kind to her inferiors; in Marion Meade, **What Fresh Hell is This?** *(1988)* •946

Nobody has any business to go around looking like horse and behaving as if it were all right. You don't catch horses going around looking like people do you? *Dorothy Parker* •947

She wore a low but futile décolletage.
Dorothy Parker •948

You mean those clothes of hers are intentional?
Dorothy Parker •949

As a source of entertainment, conviviality and good fun, she ranks somewhere between a sprig of parsley and a single ice-skate.
Dorothy Parker •950

Now to me, Edith looks like something that would eat her young. *Dorothy Parker on Edith Evans, British stage and screen actress* •951

She has only two expressions — joy and indigestion.
Dorothy Parker on film star Marion Davies •952

In fact, now that you've got me right down to it, the only thing I didn't like about 'The Barretts of Wimpole Street' was the play.
Dorothy Parker in **The New Yorker,** 1931 •953

Its hero is caused, by a novel device, to fall asleep
and a-dream; and thus he is given yesterday.
Me, I should have given him twenty years to life.
Dorothy Parker on A.A. Milne's play Give Me Yesterday, *in* The New Yorker, *1931* •954

This is not a novel to be tossed aside lightly. It should be thrown with great force.

Dorothy Parker, in R.E. Drennan, Wit's End •955

Theodore Dreiser
Should ought to write nicer.

Dorothy Parker reviewing Dawn *by Dreiser, in* The New Yorker, *May 1931* •956

And it is that word hummy, my darlings, that marks the first place in The House at Pooh Corner at which the Tonstant Weader Fwowed up.

Dorothy Parker — under the pseudonym Constant Reader — is nauseated by Pooh's hums in A.A. Milne's The House at Pooh Corner. *In* The New Yorker, *October 1928* •957

The affair between Margot Asquith and Margot Asquith will live as one of the prettiest love stories in all literature.

Dorothy Parker reviews Margot Asquith's Lay Sermons; *in* New Yorker, *22 October 1927* •958

If, with the literate, I am
Impelled to try an epigram,
I never seek to take the credit;
We all assume that Oscar said it.
Dorothy Parker, 'A Pig's-Eye View of Literature' (1937) •959

I'm just a little Jewish girl
trying to be cute.
If you say so, Dorothy •960

How can they tell?

Dorothy Parker, on being informed that Calvin Coolidge was dead •961

*This index is not intended to be comprehensive, but includes
serial wits, famous writers and subjects unfortunate enough
to have been the butt of numerable barbs.*

Redford, Robert •588-590
Reed, Rex •571, •591, •592
Richardson, Ralph •667, •668
Rivers, Joan •75, •117, •118, •511, •512, •530, •605
Robinson, Anne •44, •45
Rochester, Earl of •184, •185
Roosevelt, Eleanor •246
Roosevelt, Franklin D. •247, •248
Roosevelt, Theodore •239-242, •789
Rourke, Mickey •606
Sahl, Mort •267, •616
Sand, George •51, •773
Sartre, Jean-Paul •146
Schwarzenegger, Arnold •597, •599
Scott, Walter •746, •762
Shakespeare, William •746, •878-899
Shaw, George Bernard •71, •225, •381, •397, •413, •493, •647, •652, •746, •795-798, •921
Sheridan, R.B. •285, •286
Shulman, Milton •663, •699
Simon, John •627, •669, •671, •676
Sinatra, Frank •508, •510, •582
Sitwell, Edith •153, •813-815, •820, •826
Sledging •468-476
Smith, F.E. •2, •325, •327
Smith, Logan Pearsall •421, •812
Smith, Stevie •60
Smith, Sydney •30, •86, •214. •412, •670, •718, •760, •761
Socrates •741
Southey, Robert •770, •771
Stanwyck, Barbara •170, •563
Stein, Gertrude •809, •817, •818
Steinem, Gloria •96
Steingarten, Jeffrey •858, •864, •866
Stendahl •222
Stephenson, Pamela •152, •387
Stevenson, Adlai •231, •254, •726

Stevenson, Robert Louis •7, •779
Stoppard, Tom •219, •708, •729, •828
Streisand, Barbra •591
Swift, Jonathon •77, •131, •199, •751
Taylor, Elizabeth •604, •605
Tennyson, Alfred, Lord •719, •776, •777, •782
Thackeray, William •383, •751
Thatcher, Margaret •341-349
Thick of It •38, •69, •371
Thomas, Dylan •220, •814, •833
Thurber, James •140
Truman,, Harry S. •249, •256, •503
Twain, Mark •229, •391, •485, •706, •763, •936-941
Tynan, Kenneth •49, •119, •618-621, •653, •667, •704, •721, •736
Vidal, Gore •224, •251-253, •262, •707, •840
Voltaire •748, •752
Wagner, Richard •484-486
Walpole, Horace •743, •757
Waugh, Evelyn •148, •212, •303, •334, •806, •816, •825, •834, •838
Welles, Orson •213, •522
Wharton, Edith •720, •785
Whistler, James McNeil •160, •705, •935
Whitelaw, Willie •337, •338
Widdecombe, Ann •359, •361
Wilde, Oscar •19, •167, •414, •725, •852, •853, •920-935, •959
Wilder, Billy •566, •570, •594, •609
Williams, Kenneth •673
Williams, Robin •451, •598
Wilson, Harold •279, •332, •333
Wodehouse, P.G. •56, •64, •386, •824, •831
Wollstonecraft, Mary •757
Wood, Victoria •208
Woolf, Virginia •28, •154, •724, •788, •792-794, •808, •826
Yeats, W.B. •646, •765
Yes, Minister •362, •363.

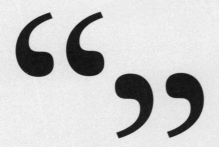